LEROY EIMS

Prayer: More Than Words

NAVPRESS
A MINISTRY OF THE NAVIGATORS
P.O. Box 6000, Colorado Springs, CO 80934

The Navigators is an international,
evangelical Christian organization. Jesus
Christ gave his followers the Great Com-
mission to go and make disciples
(Matthew 28:19). The aim of The
Navigators is to multiply laborers for
Christ in every nation, thus helping fulfill
Christ's great commission.

NavPress is the publishing ministry of
The Navigators. NavPress publications
are tools to help Christians grow.
Although publications alone cannot
make disciples or change lives, they can
help believers learn biblical discipleship
and apply what they learn to their lives
and ministries.

© 1982 by LeRoy Eims
All rights reserved, including translation
Library of Congress Catalog Card
Number:
ISBN 0-89109-493-8
14936

Printed in the United States of America.

Contents

Author

LeRoy Eims is currently serving as Assistant to the President of The Navigators. During his many years with the organization he has served in a variety of responsible positions, including Divisional Director for all the United States ministries.

For many years LeRoy has had a vital interest in winning people to Christ and building them up in the faith. He has, in fact, devoted his entire Christian life to that endeavor. LeRoy has traveled throughout the world, ministering on campuses and military bases and in churches, seminaries, and Bible schools.

LeRoy and his wife Virginia make their home in Colorado Springs and have three grown children.

Other books by LeRoy are,

Winning Ways
Be a Motivational Leader
Be the Leader You Were Meant to Be
Wisdom from Above for Living Here Below
No Magic Formula
The Lost Art of Disciple Making
What Every Christian Should Know About Growing
Disciples in Action

Preface

If you programmed a talking robot to pray without ceasing, would God listen? Suppose he prayed good prayers—scriptural prayers—using all the right words and following all the right rules. Let's say his prayers included all the various types of conversation with God, such as confession, praise, intercession, and petition. Would God pay attention to the robot's prayers? Of course not!

But wait a minute. If we say that God will not

answer a robot's prayers, we have accepted a startling proposition—*prayer is more than words!* Then what is prayer? The Bible teaches that God takes as much notice of the *person* who is praying as he does of the *words* being said.

A robot would have no power with God in prayer because it has no heart or will; it could not respond to God or obey him.

This book examines the relationship between the believer's life and his power with God in prayer. The cause for many an unanswered prayer can be traced to a disobedient or carnal life. When a Christian is disobedient, his power with God is nullified, his prayer life is crippled, and a powerful influence for good is lost to the world.

The Lord implanted this truth in my heart during a preaching ministry in Phoenix, Arizona. I was speaking on two consecutive Sundays at the Scottsdale Bible Church, and the congregation was kind enough to provide a home for my wife and me to use during the week between the two Sundays. We decided to use that week as study time. My intent was to do a Bible study on each of the eight "Imperatives for the Eighties" that The Navigators had adopted earlier that year during a meeting of our international leadership. The first imperative read, "We must strengthen our worldwide prayer emphasis, since God's Spirit blesses that which springs from the prayer of faith." The Scripture verse used to support this imperative was Matthew 21:22—"And all things, whatsoever ye shall ask in prayer, believing, ye shall receive."

I got up at dawn on Monday, had breakfast, and launched into my Bible study. By nightfall I was not done, so I continued the study on prayer Tuesday. The week ended, and I still was not past this first imperative. So I decided to continue.

For the past two years the continuing topic of my Bible study has been prayer. The study was originally for my own life, but I have occasionally shared some of it with others—Navigator staff members in Latin America and in Great Britain, students of the Baptist Student Union of the University of Oklahoma, and various Sunday school classes at my home church. The contents of this book are the result of those two years of fairly intense study.

I have not written a "how-to" book. The Lord has led me, rather, to search out the underlying principles of prayer in the Bible and to show how these principles relate to the life of the person who is praying. The focus has been on what we should *be* rather than what we should do. We will look at the biblical basis for an effective prayer life—one that has power with God.

I mentioned earlier that this study was personal—something for my own life. That is still true. Many principles mentioned here are things I am still asking God to build deeply into my prayer life.

I send this book forth with the prayer that God will use it to enhance your prayer life, as he has mine.

LeRoy Eims

Prayer: More Than Words

1
As a Son to His Father

AND HE SAID UNTO THEM,
WHEN YE PRAY, SAY, OUR FATHER
WHICH ART IN HEAVEN.

Luke 11:2

SUPPOSE YOU VISITED the local ice cream store and ordered a double-dip chocolate cone. The counter girl was quite cheerful—scooped it up, took a great big lick of your cone, handed it to you, and said, "Ummm, that chocolate is terrific!" What would your reaction be? You'd probably be shocked, appalled, surprised, offended; you might call the manager and make an issue of it.

But let's say you and your daughter visited the

3

same ice cream store a week later. You decided to have a double-dip chocolate cone, and she wanted only a medium-size cola. So you sat down in a booth while your daughter went to get the ice cream and coke. Soon she came back, plopped down in the booth with you, took a great big lick of your cone, handed it to you, and said, "Ummm, that chocolate is terrific!" What would your reaction be? You'd probably say, "Glad you liked it, Sweetie," and think nothing of it.

Why the difference? Did you suspect the counter girl had a cold or the flu? No, she looked perfectly healthy. Did you suspect she didn't brush her teeth or use scented mouthwash? No, she had a beautiful sparkling smile, just like your daughter's. Why then were you so disturbed by her licking your cone, while you had no adverse reaction at all when your daughter did the same thing? The difference is that your daughter has a relationship with you that is special. She has certain privileges that non-family members don't enjoy.

Look at this truth from another angle. Suppose that your son's birthday is coming in five days. At the dinner table he announces that he hopes you haven't forgotten his birthday and that he would sure like a new pair of jeans and a basketball for his birthday present. What would your reaction be? You'd probably reflect on the ragged condition of the jeans he was wearing and think of the fun you and he could have shooting baskets together. But suppose that after dinner the neighbor's son knocked at the door and, when you opened it, announced that his birthday was coming up in a few days and he was hoping you would buy him a new pair of jeans and a basketball. You'd probably be shocked at his audacity, especially because you know his parents could easily buy them for him.

Why the difference? Was it because you hated the kid? No, he was nice enough. Had he done something wrong—broken your window or let the air out of your tires? No, he was generally considerate of others. The only difference between him and your son was in their relationship to you. Your son had a right to talk to you about new jeans and a basketball because he was your son.

So it is with the child of God. He has certain rights and privileges that those who have never established a Father and child relationship with the Lord do not possess.

Let me enlarge on that idea. The New Testament presents God as the Father of all people in the world in the sense that he created them and provides sun and rain for their crops and flowers. But the Bible does not say that *all* people are the children of God. We become God's children when we respond to his gift of love in Jesus Christ. Galatians 3:26 defines "children of God" rather narrowly: "For ye are all the children of God by faith in Christ Jesus." Every word in that verse is important. If we read only part of it, "for ye are all the children of God," we miss the limiting phrase and could believe an error. We must also understand the last part of the verse: "by faith in Christ Jesus."

How do we become children of God? The answer is found in John 1:12,13—"But *as many as received him*, to them gave he power to become the sons of God, even to *them that believe on his name*: Which were born, not of blood, nor of the will of the flesh, nor of the will of man, but of God." Four words in this passage stand out. The first is the word *received*. We receive Christ into our lives as we would receive into our home a friend who knocked on our door. We simply open the door and invite him in. Jesus said, "Behold, I stand at the door, and knock: if any man hear my voice, and open the door, I will come in to him, and will sup with him, and he with me" (Revelation 3:20). We open our hearts to him in repentance and faith and invite him into our lives. Faith in Christ is the requirement to enter into the family of God and to receive God's promised blessings. This is why the apostle Paul prays for the Ephesians "that Christ may dwell in your hearts *by faith*" (Ephesians 3:17). He comes to dwell in our hearts when we hear his knock and bid him enter. Faith is the only means by which Christ can dwell in our lives.

The second word is *sons*, or "children." When we receive Christ, God establishes a remarkable relationship between himself and us. We actually become "partakers" of the divine nature.

The third word is *believe*, or "take him at his word." This word *believe* is crucial to understanding John's gospel. John uses the word frequently, but its most famous occurrence is in John 3:16—"For God so loved the world, that he gave his only begotten Son, that whosoever *believeth* in him should not perish, but have everlasting life." In many passages John insists that our belief, or lack of it, has awesome eternal consequences. For example, John 3:18 says, "He that believeth on him is not condemned: but he that believeth not *is condemned already*, because he hath not believed in the name of the only begotten Son of God." In John 3:36 he repeats this promise and warning: "He that believeth on the Son hath everlasting life: and he that believeth not the Son shall not see life; but the wrath of God abideth on him."

The fourth word is *born*. John emphasizes that becoming a child of God requires a spiritual birth. This birth is not something our parents can give us. Nor is it produced by the power of our own will or of the will of another. This spiritual birth does not spring from any human or earthly source. John states that this birth originates with God. It is "of God." The Holy Spirit implants spiritual life in us when we receive Christ as our Savior—when we turn from our sins and turn to him in repentance and faith. God wants us to know that we possess this "new birth" here and now: "And this is the record, that God hath given to us eternal life, and this life is in his Son. He that hath the Son hath life; and he that hath not the Son of God hath not life. These things have I written unto you that believe on the name of the Son of God; that ye may know that ye have eternal life, and that ye may believe on the name of the Son of God" (1 John 5:11-13).

As we grow into a deepening fellowship with God, we become aware of the tremendous assurances that come our way as his children. We have at least five major assurances.

First, we have *the assurance of salvation*. "Verily, verily, I say unto you, He that heareth my word, and believeth on him that sent me, *hath* [present tense] everlasting life, and shall not come into condemnation; but is passed from death unto life" (John 5:24). I have seen very little growth among Christians, very little enjoyment of the Christian life, very little usefulness in the Kingdom of God, until a person comes to this crucial assurance. The person who is plagued with doubts and fears lives in an unhealthy spiritual climate which inhibits growth, joy, and fruitfulness.

God has also given us *the assurance of victory*. "There hath no temptation taken you but such as is common to man: but God is faithful, who will not suffer you to be tempted above that ye are able; but will with the temptation also make a way to escape, that ye may be able to bear it" (1 Corinthians 10:13). We do not have to live in defeat, surrendering to the corruptions of our sinful nature, the attacks of Satan, or the allurements of the world. Spiritual victory over evil is the birthright of the healthy child of God.

Third, God gives us *the assurance of forgiveness*. Since we are living in mortal bodies, we sometimes fail to live up to the potential of our new nature. We may fail to obey the Lord, or fall into sin. But God has made perfect provision for such failure and has promised to forgive, cleanse, and restore us to fellowship with himself when we admit our failures: "If we confess our sins, he is faithful and just to forgive us our sins, and to cleanse us from all unrighteousness" (1 John 1:9).

Fourth, he has given us *the assurance of guidance*. As we walk with the Lord, God will guide us in making the right decisions and walking in the right path. In fact, God is far more interested in guiding us than we are in being guided. Psalm 48:14 declares, "This God is our God for ever and ever: he will be our guide even unto death."

Fifth, he has given us *the assurance of answered prayer*. "Hitherto have ye asked nothing in my name: ask, and ye shall receive, that your joy may be full" (John 16:24). One of the most exciting things about the Christian life is the sure knowledge that when we pray, God is listening. There is nothing more certain than the promise that the Lord hears and answers prayer. Our Father is delighted when his sons and daughters come to him with their petitions. He is grieved, just as any parent is grieved, when his child distrusts him, is cold toward him, is afraid of him, or treats him like a stranger.

As we reflect on our privileges as God's children, we must not forget the responsibilities that go along with them.

A couple of years ago my wife and I bought a new clothes dryer. We checked a few stores and finally decided which dryer met our needs and fit our budget. The salesman was enthusiastic about this particular dryer. He had sold many of this model, and he hadn't received one complaint. It seemed to run for many years without a breakdown. It was fairly inexpensive. It had a little buzzer that sounded when the load was dry. The store would deliver it free and set it up where we wanted it. The store also had its own service department. We were sold!

But then the salesman began to talk about our obligations. It would require so much money for a down payment. We had to sign a contract agreeing to pay so much each month for a specified amount of time. There was a warranty with the dryer, but it would not be honored if we violated certain rules and regulations.

We quickly found there were two sides to this contract. Owning this dryer brought us great privileges and advantages, but it also brought with it definite responsibilities.

As you study the Bible you find that some of your responsibilities as a child of God demand sacrifice. It is not all easy. Look at three of these obligations.

In Matthew 5:43–48, Jesus tells us to *love our enemies*:

> Ye have heard that it hath been said, Thou shalt love thy neighbour, and hate thine enemy. But I say unto you, Love your enemies, bless them that curse you, do good to them that hate you, and pray for them which despitefully use you and persecute you; That ye may be the children of your Father which is in heaven: for he maketh his sun to rise on the evil and on the good, and sendeth rain on the just and on the unjust. For if ye love them which love you, what reward have ye? do not even the publicans the same? And if ye salute your brethren only, what do ye more *than others*? do not even the publicans so? Be ye therefore perfect, even as your Father which is in heaven is perfect.

This command seems impossibly hard. Anybody can love a person who loves him. But love your enemies? Why should we do this? Jesus says it is proof that you are a child of your Father in Heaven. In loving those who love you there is no evidence that you are any different from the worst of men. Practically anyone is able to show love to people of his own nationality, social class, political persuasion, and religion. Jesus, however, calls upon us to speak well of our *enemies*, to do good to them, and to pray for them. That's what he did. On the cross he prayed for those who were murdering him, "Father, forgive them; for they know not what they do" (Luke 23:34). God also shows his love to those who hate him by sending sun and rain to them exactly as he does to his children. He has left us an example. When we forgive our enemies and do good to them, as he does, the watching world will note that we are the children of our heavenly father.

Our second responsibility is to *become mature Christians*. The apostle Peter says that if we are the sons and daughters of God we will grow in the family likeness: "As obedient children, not fashioning yourselves according to the former lusts in your ignorance: But as he which hath called you is holy, so be ye holy in all manner of conversation; Because it is written, Be ye holy; for I am holy" (1 Peter 1:14–16). We must not pattern our conduct after our old life but mold our character after the likeness of our Father in heaven. God is absolutely holy. His character, motives, and works are perfect. To imitate God, however, does not mean we must become perfect. He does not ask the impossible. He does ask us, though, to make obedience to the word of God our lifestyle and to trust the Holy Spirit to produce in us the family likeness.

The person who is seeking God, but who also realizes his failures, can take comfort from Ephesians 5:1—"Be ye therefore followers of God, as dear children." It used to trouble me that the Bible set such a high standard. Imitate God! How could I as a human being do that? I can't even imitate Bing Crosby or Billy Graham. But notice the words, "as dear children."

My daughter Becky loves to listen to her daughter read, even though Joy does not read as well as Becky does. Becky doesn't expect her to. Becky loves to watch her daughter Amber Lynn learn to walk. She doesn't walk as well as Becky— even on flat surfaces—but she is learning to walk by imitating her mother. Nor is she as neat and proper when she eats. But she is learning. As her mother's "dear child," she is imitating her parent. And as the years go on, she will grow more and more like her mother and take on the characteristics of the family. The family likeness will become evident.

Just as little children learn to read and walk and eat by imitating their parents, so you and I learn holiness by imitating our Father in heaven.

Third, we are to *shine in the world*. "Do all things without murmurings and disputings: That ye may be blameless and harmless, the sons of God, without rebuke, in the midst of a crooked and perverse nation, among whom ye shine as lights in the world" (Philippians 2:14–15). We shine through cheerful obedience to the word of God (without murmuring) and by getting along well with our fellow man (without disputing). But such conduct is not humanly possible. Galatians 4:6 gives the secret of a shining lifestyle: "And because ye are sons, God hath sent forth the Spirit of his Son into your hearts, crying, Abba, Father." The indwelling Holy Spirit gives us the power to live the Christian life.

Hebrews 12:6–7 teaches that God disciplines his children: "For whom the Lord loveth he chasteneth, and scourgeth every son whom he receiveth. If ye endure chastening, God dealeth with you as with sons; for what son is he whom the father chasteneth not?" The discipline of God proves his fatherly love for his children and proves that they are his own.

When our son Randy was eleven years old, he got into some trouble. He stole our neighbors' outdoor Christmas lights. He and a neighbor kid took them all down to the bridge near our home and threw them against the cement to hear them pop. They thought it was great fun. Naturally, when I found out about it, I disciplined Randy. But I did not discipline the neighbor boy, because he was not my child. God's discipline in our lives proves that we are his children.

The apostle Paul says that because we have been received into the family of God "we cry, Abba, Father" (Romans 8:15). It is natural for a baby to cry. God expects his children to do it. He delights to hear their cry, and he blesses them when they cry out to him. So, Christian, because you are a child of God, accepted in the family, cry. Cry to him. Pour out your heart. Your Father will hear and answer your prayer.

2
Prayer and the Bible

IF YE ABIDE IN ME,
AND MY WORDS ABIDE IN YOU,
YE SHALL ASK WHAT YE WILL,
AND IT SHALL BE DONE UNTO YOU.

John 15:7

WE COULDN'T BELIEVE it. It had all started the night before when the phone rang. My wife and I were staying in the home of a family who were co-laborers with us in the Navigator ministry. When Kees answered the phone, he seemed quite concerned. He hung up the phone and told us he and his wife would have to leave for a while. The child of friends of theirs was very ill, and the parents had called to ask them to come over to their home and

16

pray for the sick child. They left, and my wife and I went to our bedroom and retired for the night.

The next morning, as we were sitting around the breakfast table, I asked them how it had gone at their friends' home. They said it was awful. Shortly after they arrived, the pastor of the nearby church came. He would not let them pray for the child and would not pray himself. He didn't believe in prayer.

As we discussed the situation, the problem became evident. The church had departed from the Bible. Most of its recent pastors had had very little to do with the word of God. They didn't believe it. They didn't preach it. They substituted man's wisdom for the wisdom of God. And because they no longer believed the Bible, they no longer believed in prayer. They had no basis for prayer because they had no promises to claim. Their prayer lives had evaporated. That church today knows nothing of the power that comes from calling on God by faith in the name of Christ.

As a consequence a child lay sick that night while those who stood by his bed were forbidden to unite in prayer. Conclusion: When a person neglects his Bible, he loses confidence in it, then feels himself superior to it; subsequently his prayer life weakens and dies.

In the early 1960s my wife and I were involved in a collegiate ministry in the Midwest. Two of the young men who were with us in the ministry suffered a severe setback in their Christian life and service. Their decline began when they decided to take a religion course at the university. Day after day this course eroded their faith. The professor did not believe the Bible. The textbooks he used in the class were written by men and women who did not believe the Bible. The faith of our two young friends was shaken and finally shattered. Their lives lost their spiritual luster. Doubt and unbelief replaced faith. Their prayer life was ruined. Questions plagued their thoughts. How could they know God would hear them? How could they know God would act? How could they know God wanted them to pray? Without the Bible, prayer became pointless.

John 15:7 teaches that prayer and the Bible must go hand in hand: "If ye abide in me, and my words abide in you, ye shall ask what ye will, and it shall be done unto you." Note carefully the words, "ask what ye will." There seems to be no boundary here, no limitation to what we can ask. But there is a boundary—the will of God.

In previous conversations with his disciples, Christ had spoken about *his* abiding in the believer. Here he changes from speaking about *his* abiding in the believer to *his words* abiding in the believer. This significant progression of thought throws light on the relationship between the Bible and prayer. If Christ's words abide in us and we are yielded to the truth of his word, our requests will be in harmony with the will of God. Every thought will be "brought into captivity to the obedience of Christ" (2 Corinthians 10:5).

As our prayer lives are molded by the word of Christ to the will of God, we can pray with confidence: "And this is the confidence that we have in him, that, if we ask anything according to his will, he heareth us: And if we know that he hear us, whatsoever we ask, we know that we have the petitions that we desired of him" (1 John 5:14–15).

If we want God to bless our prayer life, we must heed the admonition of the apostle Paul: "Let the word of Christ dwell in you richly in all wisdom; teaching and admonishing one another in psalms and hymns and spiritual songs, singing with grace in your hearts to the Lord" (Colossians 3:16). If the word is to dwell richly in our hearts, it must be there as more than a guest in a house; it must dwell there as the master of the house with a right to govern what goes on under his roof. We must be under its authority. And, if it is to dwell *richly* within, it must dwell *in abundance*. The Spirit of God uses the word of God to direct our conduct and lead us in the paths of righteousness. It is not enough for us to have read it a little here and there and to have memorized a verse or two.

Christ wants to transform our lives. He wants

to deepen our prayer life, to help us become true prayer warriors, good soldiers in his army. Our objective is to destroy the works of the devil. We can achieve this victory only as we transform Christ's promises into prayer and lay them at the throne of grace.

The Old Testament also clearly states that the Bible and prayer are inseparable. "He that turneth away his ear from hearing the law, even his prayer shall be abomination" (Proverbs 28:9).

It is through the Scriptures and prayer that our fellowship with God is maintained. If we willfully neglect or disobey the word of God, our prayers, which should delight the Lord, will instead be an abomination to him. We cannot expect that God will answer our prayers if, while we are calling to him, we refuse to listen to him call to us through his word. God made it plain through the prophet Zechariah why the people's prayers were not answered:

> Yea, they made their hearts as an adamant stone, lest they should hear the law, and the words which the Lord of hosts hath sent in his spirit by the former prophets: therefore came a great wrath from the Lord of hosts. Therefore it is come to pass, that as he cried, and they would not hear; so they cried, and I would not hear, saith the Lord of hosts. (Zechariah 7:12–13)

When we turn a deaf ear to God's word, he turns a deaf ear to our prayers.

> Because I have called, and ye refused; I have stretched out my hand, and no man regarded; But ye have set at nought all my counsel, and would none of my reproof. . . . Then shall they call upon me, but I will not answer; they shall seek me early, but they shall not find me: For that they hated knowledge, and did not choose the fear of the Lord: They would none of my counsel: they despised all my reproof. (Proverbs 1:24–25, 28–30)

The word of God is vital to our prayer life. Consider a few passages from both the Old and New Testaments that show its value:

> I have manifested thy name unto the men which thou gavest me out of the world: thine they were, and thou gavest them me; and *they have kept thy word*. . . . I have given them *thy word*, and the world hath hated them, because they are not of the world, even as I am not of the world. . . . Sanctify them through thy truth: *thy word* is truth. (John 17:6, 14, 17)

Jesus prays for the sanctification of his disciples through the word of God. He calls it *"thy* truth." He is not speaking of truth in general, or even of religious truth in particular. He is speaking of his Father's truth—*revealed* truth. He is speaking of the Old Testament, the part of the Bible that existed then. Prophetically, however, he is referring to the entire Bible, Old and New Testaments, as the means of future saints being set apart to God for his purposes.

As he expanded and interpreted the Old Testament, Jesus frequently referred to it as the revelation of himself:

> And he said unto them, These are the words
> which I spake unto you, while I was yet with
> you, that all things must be fulfilled, which were
> written in the law of Moses, and in the prophets,
> and in the psalms, concerning me. (Luke 24:44)

It was the Old Testament, he said, that bore testimony to himself (see John 5:39–40). The apostle Paul also refers to the "gospel of God, Which he had promised afore *by his prophets* in the holy scriptures" (Romans 1:1–2).

Through the Bible we learn what God wants us to do and how to do it. It is "entire truth." It has no deficiency. It is the full and final revelation of all that God wants us to know.

One aspect of Christ's transfiguration may be instructive here. Peter, James, and John went with Jesus to a high mountain. Jesus was transfigured before them, and the three saw Moses and Elijah talking with Christ. While they were at the mountain, the voice of God the Father spoke to them, and Jesus spoke to them, but Moses and Elijah did not. Some Bible students have suggested that they could not speak because their words had already been recorded in the Old Testament, and the Old Testament revelation was complete. Nothing could be taken from it or added to it. Whatever Peter, James, and John would learn from Moses and Elijah they would learn through the Scriptures.

Although this illustration is speculative, the principle of God's revelation being complete in written form in the Bible is not speculative. The church has always recognized that the canon of Scripture, both Old and New Testaments, was completed in the first century when John, the last of the apostles, wrote the book of Revelation. In this last book of the Bible the apostle John sternly forbids anyone to add to or subtract from the *"words* of the prophecy of this book." John was no doubt referring specifically to the book of Revelation, but it is significant that this warning occurs in the last book in the canon of Scripture.

Many heretical groups and sects since the first century A.D. have claimed to have received a further revelation from God. Most of these later "revelations" contradict passages of the Bible. The Old Testament sets forth a rule which was to be applied to any utterance pretending to be a prophecy from God: "To the law and to the testimony: if they speak not according to this word, it is because there is no light in them" (Isaiah 8:20). The Bible is the standard that judges the truthfulness of all other statements. We do not have to sit expectantly waiting for the next word from God. We've got it all in the Bible.

The word of God guides our conduct; apart from Scripture we go astray. At one point, Jesus blamed the murderous intent of the Jews on their failure to receive his word. "I know that ye are Abraham's seed; but ye seek to kill me, because my word hath no place in you" (John 8:37). They were about to commit the horrible sin of murder because Christ's word had no "place" in them. This passage is translated in various ways: "My teaching makes no headway with you" (*The New English Bible*); "You have no room for my word" (*New International Version*); "My word has no entrance—makes no progress, does not find any place—in you" (*The Amplified Bible*); "My message does not find a home in your hearts" (*The Living Bible*). I have listed these various translations because of the powerful truth they contain. Christ told the Jews his word had not penetrated them.

Isaiah compares God's word to rain falling upon the earth:

For as the rain cometh down, and the snow from heaven, and returneth not thither, but watereth

the earth, and maketh it bring forth and bud,
that it may give seed to the sower, and bread to
the eater: So shall my word be that goeth forth
out of my mouth: it shall not return unto me
void, but it shall accomplish that which I please,
and it shall prosper in the thing whereto I sent it.
(Isaiah 55:10–11)

On the farm in Iowa we always welcomed the
April showers. The thirsty ground would soak up
the rain. But at our present home in Colorado
Springs when the rains come, most of the water
simply runs down the road. It cannot penetrate the
asphalt that covers the street.

Jesus was telling his would-be murderers that
their hearts were like rock that could not be penetrated. The word was not working in them because
it did not reach their consciences and wills. The
Christian must be aware of this danger and avoid a
hardened conscience. Our hearts must be open and
responsive to the word of God like the Iowa soil to
the spring rain. Satan will try to nullify its power in
our lives. But eager obedience to the Scriptures
gives God a beachhead in our lives, through which
he can influence our thoughts and actions. Jesus
acknowledged that the Jews were physical descen-
dants of Abraham, but he said they had no spiritual
kinship with him. Their lack of faith and their rejection of his word proved their spiritual alienation.

Proverbs 22:17–21 teaches that receiving God's word will bring us blessing and wisdom:

> Bow down thine ear, and hear the words of the wise, and apply thine heart unto my knowledge. For it is a pleasant thing if thou keep them within thee; they shall withal be fitted in thy lips. That thy trust may be in the Lord, I have made known to thee this day, even to thee. Have not I written to thee excellent things in counsels and knowledge, That I might make thee know the certainty of the words of truth; that thou mightest answer the words of truth to them that send unto thee?

The "excellent things" have to do with God's glory, our happiness, and the good of the human race. God's motive in giving these instructions is not to make us miserable, but to *do us good*. Furthermore, God's word speaks to us in a personal and timely way, as verse 19 points out: "I have made known to thee *this* day, even *to thee*." The message from the Lord is *to thee—this day*. Believe God *today*. Love God *today*. Obey God *today*.

To meditate on the Scriptures brings great joy to God's people. The prophet Jeremiah stated it this way: "Thy words were found, and I did eat them; and thy word was unto me the joy and rejoicing of mine heart: for I am called by thy name, O Lord God of hosts" (Jeremiah 15:16).

A response of faith and obedience to God's word will also lead to a life of holiness before the Lord. Dawson Trotman, founder of The Navigators, used to quote the saying, "God's word will keep you from sin, or sin will keep you from God's word." This statement is based on the words of the Psalmist, "Thy word have I hid in mine heart, that I might not sin against thee" (Psalm 119:11). The temptation to sin can come at any time and in any place. The great weapon of the child of God against the temptation is the Bible. When the Bible is memorized, it is available for the Holy Spirit to apply in our lives at any time and in any place.

The warnings and promises God gives in his word provide the Christian with all he needs—light when he is in the dark, strength when he is weary, companionship when he is lonely. When you consciously saturate your mind with the Scriptures and regard them as the authoritative guide for your life, you will sense their influence throughout your total personality—mind, affections, and will. Jesus told his enemies that their problem was that God's word had not permeated their lives; therefore they were embarked on a course of sin.

While in Australia, my wife and I were horrified to read this account of human sacrifice:

New Delhi: A three-year-old tribal girl had been sacrificed in a coal hearth in a village in the cen-

tral Indian state of Madhyapradesh, the home
minister, Mr. Tripathi, told the state assembly in
Bhopal on Friday. The girl had been covered
with logs and set on fire in Bhunjarai village,
southeast of Bhopal, he claimed. A goat also had
been sacrificed in the hearth.

As I read that article, it occurred to me that the
tribe's behavior was due to the same ignorance of
God's word that afflicted Jesus' murderers. Had
they known and obeyed the Bible, that little girl
could be alive today.

Thus far we have seen that the Bible is authoritative, and that it is the full and complete
revelation of God. The Holy Spirit will apply the
Scripture to our lives to keep us from sin and enable
us to serve God rightly. The words of Moses fur-
nish a summary statement:

> Therefore shall ye lay up these my words in your
> heart and in your soul, and bind them for a sign
> upon your hand, that they may be as frontlets
> between your eyes. And ye shall teach them
> your children, speaking of them when thou sit-
> test in thine house, and when thou walkest by
> the way, when thou liest down, and when thou
> risest up. (Deuteronomy 11:18–19)

He urged that our hearts and minds be filled and
our conversation salted with the word of God.

In today's world we are constantly reminded of the need for good nutrition. We are warned to stay away from junk food that will rot our teeth, fatten us, and deny us the vitamins and minerals we need to keep healthy. All well and good. But the body is temporal; the soul is eternal. In all our efforts to maintain good *physical* health, let us not neglect our *spiritual* health. We must stay spiritually strong, and we cannot do that without the Bible. It is God's appointed means to nourish our spiritual lives. Nothing can take its place. Without it we get spiritually sick.

The great men and women in the Bible have freely confessed their hunger for God's word, their dependence on it, and their determination to feed upon it day by day. Job was such a man: "Neither have I gone back from the commandment of his lips; I have esteemed the words of his mouth more than my necessary food" (Job 23:12). It would have been easier for him to live without eating than to neglect God's word.

David was certainly a man of God's word. There is no more pointed testimony to the Bible's place in our lives than Psalm 19:7–11:

> The law of the Lord is perfect, converting the soul: the testimony of the Lord is sure, making wise the simple. The statutes of the Lord are right, rejoicing the heart: the commandment of

the Lord is pure, enlightening the eyes. The fear of the Lord is clean, enduring forever: the judgments of the Lord are true and righteous altogether. More to be desired are they than gold, yea, than much fine gold: sweeter also than honey and the honeycomb. Moreover by them is thy servant warned: and in keeping of them there is great reward.

Pure—without any defilement. *Clean*—and therefore able to cleanse us. "Now ye are clean through the word which I have spoken unto you" (John 15:3). *True*—as God is true. *Righteous altogether*—announcing equity and justice to the world. David found the Scriptures more valuable than gold, more pleasurable than the sweetest delights of the world; in them he found the warnings he needed to enable him to fulfill his duties and avoid the pitfalls of life.

Why did David so highly regard the influence of God's word in his daily life? The answer can be found in 1 Chronicles 10:13–14:

So Saul died for his transgression which he committed against the Lord, even against the word of the Lord, which he kept not, and also for asking counsel of one that had a familiar spirit, to enquire of it; And *enquired not of the Lord*: therefore, he slew him, and turned the kingdom unto David, the son of Jesse.

David had seen what happened to Saul when he turned his back on the word of God and prayer. Saul died for his sin of neglecting God's word and refusing to pray. When David took Saul's place on the throne of Israel, his determination to maintain a prayer life based on the word of the Lord was surely due, at least in part, to Saul's tragic example.

We never outgrow our need for the Bible. God's word must have a vital place in the life of the new Christian as well as in the life of the mature saint. The apostle John makes this point:

> I write unto you, little children, because your sins are forgiven you for his name's sake. I write unto you, fathers, because ye have known him that is from the beginning. I write unto you, young men, because ye have overcome the wicked one. (1 John 2:12–13)

First, John addresses new babes in Christ. They are learning to fellowship with God and are experiencing the first principles of the walk of obedience and faith. Last, he speaks to the young men, those who have some spiritual muscle and are engaged in the warfare against the devil. They have become strong overcomers because they have the word of God abiding in them. Second, in between the babes and the young men, he addresses the fathers of the Christian faith, men of wisdom and experience.

The prophet Malachi speaks about a man in this group of fathers of the faith:

> The law of truth was in his mouth, and iniquity was not found in his lips: he walked with me in peace and equity, and did turn many away from iniquity. For the priest's lips should keep knowledge, and they should seek the law at his mouth: for he is the messenger of the Lord of hosts. (Malachi 2:6–7)

God has instructions for those who instruct. Paul told Timothy, "Study to shew thyself approved unto God, a workman that needeth not to be ashamed, rightly dividing the word of truth" (2 Timothy 2:15). The word that Timothy was to preach "in season and out" (2 Timothy 4:2) was the "word of truth." It takes diligent study and care to preach the word of God properly. The primary purpose of Bible study is to find out what pleases God and to do it.

The words of Jesus are clear. "If my words abide in you, ask what ye will." This promise reminds us again of the unbreakable bond between prayer and the word of God. People who neglect the Bible while continuing to pray can grow indolent and dreamy, and those who neglect prayer while continuing to study the Scriptures can become hard and brittle. We need both prayer and the Bible. Let us not neglect either one.

3
Reverence

EXALT YE THE LORD OUR GOD,
AND WORSHIP AT HIS FOOTSTOOL;
FOR HE IS HOLY.

Psalm 99:5

LET'S SUPPOSE YOU fall off a bridge. It is night.
The water is ice cold. You panic; you are a poor
swimmer, and you can feel yourself being pulled
under by the current of the river and the weight of
your clothing. Your shoes fill with water. Your
overcoat is watersoaked. You know this is the end.
Then, to your amazement, you see a man leap off
the bridge. He swims to you and pulls you to shore.
You are saved.

You both lie exhausted on the riverbank for a while, and then he takes you by the arm, helps you back up to the road, puts you in his car, and takes you to his home. All the way you are trying to express your gratitude to him. You arrive at his home, pull into a three-car garage, and for the first time you notice the car you are riding in is a top-of-the-line Cadillac. As you get out of the car you stare at the other two cars—a Mercedes-Benz and a Porsche. When you enter the house, the servants surround you, hurry you to a bedroom, and provide you with a hot shower and dry clothing. They take you to the study, where there is a warm fire in the fireplace and a hot meal waiting. You are stunned by the beauty and opulence of this home. Huge crystal chandeliers. Thick carpets. Magnificent furniture. It is obviously the home of a very wealthy individual. The owner does everything he can to make you comfortable and, later on, personally takes you home to your little three-room apartment.

If you spoke to others about this man, what would be the tone of your remarks? Would you speak of him as some guy who happened along and helped you out of a jam? Or would there be a touch of awe and respect in your remarks? In view of the man's kindness, courage, and obvious affluence, you would probably speak about him differently than you would your next-door neighbor. And when he occasionally called you on the phone to ask about your health and to see if there was anything more he could do for you, you would speak to him with an air of courtesy and respect.

Picture a man who has been out of work for months. Day after day he hits the streets answering help-wanted ads, but to no avail. Then one day he is interviewed by a lady in the personnel department of a large company. She is interested in his background and qualifications. After an in-depth interview she tells him to wait for a few minutes. The man is on pins and needles. His hope, which has been dashed so many times in recent weeks, begins to rise. He begins to perspire. His heart beats faster. His palms get wet, and his throat gets dry. Soon the lady returns and asks him to come with her. The boss wants to talk with him. Did she say the boss *himself*? Yes, the owner of the company, Mr. Big. How do you think the man walks into that office? Do you think he breezes in, tosses his hat at the hat rack, blows a cloud of smoke from his cigar, and says, "Hi ya, big shot"? Or do you think he goes in humbly, grateful for the boss's consideration, and awed at the thought of meeting the big man himself?

These two stories relate to a modern attitude toward prayer that I believe is unhealthy. It is true that God is a loving Father and that prayer is personal communication with a God who wants us to call on him. But when the Bible says to come *boldly* to the throne of grace, it does not mean *brashly*. We should not breeze into the presence of almighty God with a cocky little "Hi, there!" The very thought that the creator of heaven and earth, and the sea and all that it contains, should ever *permit* people like us to come into his presence should fill us with a sense of gratitude, awe, and reverence. Yes, he is our Father, but there should be something more than a casual "Hi ya, Pop!" when we come before him. Prayer may become so formal and ceremonial that it is not real, but it may also become so casual that it is not real. The Bible requires a balance between these two extremes.

Psalm 111:9 says God's name is "reverend." "He sent redemption unto his people: he hath commanded his covenant for ever: holy and *reverend* is his name." In this passage three things are mentioned: God's redemption, his covenant, and his name. The name of God is holy and reverend.

Most of us understand the first three-fourths of this verse. We know about redemption—that Christ redeemed us by dying in our place on the cross to free us from bondage to sin and Satan, and that we are justified—declared righteous by God— through faith in Christ alone. We know also that God is holy, free from all taint of evil, and full of moral perfection.

But do we know what the Bible means when it

says that his name is "reverend"? Does reverence mean a warm sentimental attachment, such as we might have toward an old family heirloom or a prized possesion? No, the word *reverence* has its root in the word *fear*. Thus David remarks in the next verse: "The fear of the Lord is the beginning of wisdom: a good understanding have all they that do his commandments: his praise endureth for ever" (Psalm 111:10).

A reverent fear of God will lead us to a lifestyle of obedience and praise. Psalm 89:6-7 develops this theme: "For who in the heaven can be compared unto the Lord? who among the sons of the mighty can be likened unto the Lord? God is greatly to be feared in the assembly of the saints, and to be had in reverence of all them that are about him."

What or who can be compared to the greatness, the power, or the majesty of God? Man's puny achievements, and even creation itself, pale into insignificance in comparison to God's grandeur. Attempting to compare God with anything he has created is akin to likening Victoria Falls to the faucet in the kitchen sink or the space shuttle Columbia to a child's plastic airplane. The humbling vision of the eternal and holy God stooping to help finite, sinful man prompted the writer of Hebrews to say, "Wherefore . . . let us have grace whereby we may serve God acceptably with reverence and godly fear: For our God is a consuming fire" (Hebrews 12:28–29). You and I cannot truly worship God, come to him in prayer, or serve him without feeling humbled.

There is a parallel truth which reinforces the idea that we need healthy reverence and godly fear as we approach God. The Bible teaches that all believers are priests unto God (Revelation 1:5–6); but even the priest must not presume upon God. In the Old Testament the sons of Aaron the priest entered irreverently into the presence of God and died for their presumption:

> And Nadab and Abihu, the sons of Aaron, took either of them his censer, and put fire therein, and put incense thereon, and offered strange fire before the Lord, which he commanded them not. And there went out fire from the Lord, and devoured them, and they died before the Lord. Then Moses said unto Aaron, This is it that the Lord spake, saying, I will be sanctified in them that come nigh me, and before all the people I will be glorified. And Aaron held his peace. (Leviticus 10:1–3)

What was their sin? We know from Luke 1:8–9 that the priest was permitted to burn incense before God only when it was his turn to do so. And the instructions were for the priest to do this alone. These two young priests went presumptuously into the presence of God, disregarding God's prescribed method of approaching him.

There is a lesson here for us. When we come near to God in prayer we must "sanctify" God in our hearts—set him apart as holy in our affections. Such reverence on our part will produce in us true humility. When we approach God in this way, we are accepted as God's confident and privileged children. Hebrews 10:19-22 points out this blessed paradox:

> Having therefore, brethren, boldness to enter into the holiest by the blood of Jesus, By a new and living way, which he hath consecrated for us, through the veil, that is to say, his flesh; And having an high priest over the house of God; Let us draw near with a true heart in full assurance of faith, having our hearts sprinkled from an evil conscience, and our bodies washed with pure water.

You and I enter the presence of God by a new way—a living way. Christ shed his blood to enable us to approach God in full assurance of faith. *But we must not come to him carelessly.*

Reverence speaks of an *attitude* of humility and expectation (Psalm 62:5). Some years ago there was a popular song that epitomized the careless spirit that cost Aaron's sons their lives. The song asked the question, "Have you talked to the man upstairs?" This is the spirit of our age. But calling to God is not like going out to the stairs in the apartment building where you live and calling to the landlord on the top floor.

An incident in 1 Samuel 6:1–21 teaches this same lesson. The Philistines had captured the ark of God and kept it for seven months. It brought them nothing but trouble. Chapter five records their decision to get rid of it.

> So they sent and gathered together all the lords of the Philistines, and said, Send away the ark of the God of Israel, and let it go again to his own place, that it slay us not, and our people: for there was a deadly destruction throughout all the city; the hand of God was very heavy there.
> (verse 11)

They loaded the ark on a cart, got two milk cows, took their calves away from them, hitched the cows to the wagon, and started them down the road to Bethshemesh. The cows went their way—turning neither to the right nor to the left until they arrived at their God-appointed destination. Those of us who grew up on a farm know that this simple story is really a miracle. In the first place it is not natural for cows to leave their calves. It is also strange that they would adapt so easily to a yoke, and that they would head straight as an arrow to Bethshemesh. God was obviously controlling these dumb beasts.

Upon receiving the ark, the Levites did the proper thing:

> And the Levites took down the ark of the Lord, and the coffer that was with it, wherein the jewels of gold were, and put them on the great stone: and the men of Bethshemesh offered burnt offerings and sacrificed sacrifices the same day unto the Lord. (1 Samuel 6:15)

But then they made a terrible mistake; they opened the ark.

> And he smote the men of Bethshemesh, because they had looked into the ark of the Lord, even he smote of the people fifty thousand and three-score and ten men; and the people lamented, because the Lord had smitten many of the people with a great slaughter. (1 Samuel 6:19)

Why did they open the ark? They knew that even the High Priest himself was not allowed to look at it, except once a year; even then the ark would be semi-hidden in a cloud of incense. But there is something perverse about human nature that makes people want to do things that are forbidden. Publishers know it used to be that when a book was banned, its sales increased. Possibly the men of Bethshemesh were simply curious. They wanted to take a peek, even though God had forbidden it. Or perhaps familiarity with the things of

God had so bred contempt and irreverence that these men went too far and paid for their disobedience with their lives.

What lesson can we learn from this incident? The Psalmist says the power and holiness of God command respect:

> The Lord reigneth; let the people tremble: he sitteth between the cherubims; let the earth be moved. The Lord is great in Zion; and he is high above all the people. Let them praise thy great and terrible name; for it is holy. The king's strength also loveth judgment; thou dost establish equity, thou executest judgment and righteousness in Jacob. Exalt ye the Lord our God, and worship at his footstool; for he is holy. Moses and Aaron among his priests, and Samuel among them that call upon his name; they called upon the Lord, and he answered them. He spake unto them in the cloudy pillar: they kept his testimonies, and the ordinance that he gave them. Thou answeredst them, O Lord our God: thou wast a God that forgavest them, though thou tookest vengeance of their inventions. Exalt the Lord our God, and worship at his holy hill; for the Lord our God is holy. (Psalm 99)

In each of these verses we are commanded to praise, exalt, and worship the Lord. Why? In verse one he tells us "The Lord reigneth." God is King.

The universe is at his command. The thought of God's omnipotence should shock our thinking and cause us to exalt the Lord.

I recall an incident in which the simple biblical truth of God's sovereignty had a sobering effect. I was standing outside the Outrigger Hotel on Waikiki Beach in Honolulu, waiting for the Navigator representative to come by in his car to take me to preach to a group of servicemen. All of a sudden a drunk came lurching up to me, waved a handful of money in my face, and declared, "This rules the world!" Without giving it a great deal of thought, I turned to him, waved my Bible in his face, and said, "You're wrong. God rules the world." He took one look at that Bible and immediately changed his tune. "Of course," he said, "I know that. I'm a good churchgoer," and he began trying to convince me of his true religious nature. I was not impressed, and I'm sure God wasn't either.

But it's true, isn't it? God rules the world. And on the basis of that awesome fact the Psalmist tells us to "exalt the Lord and worship at his footstool."

A true vision of God's exalted greatness cannot help but produce feelings of profound humility in us. I cannot stand in the presence of the Lord without being painfully conscious of my own insignificance. The other side of exalting the Lord is humbling myself.

Closely allied to God's omnipotence is his

holiness—his spotless purity, his unswerving justice, his absolute truth. Moses asks the question, "Who is like unto thee, O Lord, among the gods? Who is like thee, *glorious in holiness*, fearful in praises, doing wonders?" (Exodus 15:11). The Egyptians, and many other pagan nations, had a myriad of gods who were often cruel, passionate, and inconsistent, just as men often are. Often the great men of the earth looked upon themselves as gods. But Moses exalts the Lord to a place of infinite greatness in comparison to them.

The prophet Isaiah combines these two attributes, omnipotence and holiness, in a graphic picture of God:

> In the year that king Uzziah died I saw also the Lord sitting upon a throne, high and lifted up, and his train filled the temple. Above it stood the seraphims: each one had six wings; with twain he covered his face, and with twain he covered his feet, and with twain he did fly. And one cried unto another, and said, Holy, holy, holy, is the Lord of hosts: the whole earth is full of his glory. (Isaiah 6:1–3)

Isaiah's reaction to this vision of God's holiness was one of deep unworthiness: "Then said I, Woe is me! for I am undone; because I am a man of unclean lips, and I dwell in the midst of a people of unclean lips" (Isaiah 6:5).

Humility is an integral part of reverence in the
presence of God's holiness. Malachi speaks of the
universal reverence that God will one day receive:

> For from the rising of the sun even unto the go-
> ing down of the same my name shall be great
> among the Gentiles; and in every place incense
> shall be offered unto my name, and a pure offer-
> ing: for my name shall be great among the
> heathen, saith the Lord of hosts. (Malachi 1:11)

From every part of the world disciples will arise
who will exalt and revere God's name.

Revelation 5:9 pictures the fulfillment of that
prophecy: "And they sung a new song, saying,
Thou art *worthy* to take the book, and to open the
seals thereof: for thou wast slain, and hast redeemed us to God by thy blood out of every kin-
dred, and tongue, and people, and nation." The
chapter ends with an exhilarating climax:

> And I beheld, and I heard the voice of many
> angels round about the throne and the beasts
> and the elders: and the number of them was ten
> thousand times ten thousand, and thousands of
> thousands; Saying with a loud voice, Worthy is
> the Lamb that was slain to receive power, and
> riches, and wisdom, and strength, and honor,
> and glory, and blessing. And every creature
> which is in heaven, and on the earth, and under

the earth, and such as are in the sea, and all that are in them, heard I saying, Blessing, and honor, and glory, and power, be unto him that sitteth upon the throne, and unto the Lamb for ever and ever. And the four beasts said, Amen. And the four and twenty elders fell down and worshipped him that liveth for ever and ever. (Revelation 5:11–14)

That is a picture of reverence—profound humility and godly fear in the awesome presence of God.

Fix that magnificent picture in your mind, and then think about this question: One day you will be ushered into the presence of our omnipotent and holy God. How do you picture that moment? Do you see yourself sauntering into his presence preoccupied with secondary things? I'm sure that's not the case. Here's the point: Whatever attitude you see yourself manifesting in that day will guide your spirit today. If you see yourself in an attitude of profound reverence *then*, let a spirit of profound reverence prevail *now* as you daily approach the throne of grace in prayer to your loving heavenly Father, the Lord God Almighty.

4
Obedience

AND WHATSOEVER WE ASK,
WE RECEIVE OF HIM, BECAUSE WE
KEEP HIS COMMANDMENTS,
AND DO THOSE THINGS THAT ARE
PLEASING IN HIS SIGHT.

1 John 3:22

ON JULY 4, 1981, the Colorado Springs *Gazette-Telegraph* announced the escape of Albert the Alligator from the Denver Zoo. Albert, who had been missing for fifteen days, was now living in nearby Duck Lake, where visitors began gathering to catch a glimpse of him. Zoo officials in diving suits and speed boats tried to recapture Albert, but he managed to evade them. Trying to bait Albert with food was useless, because the lake was full of

fish—carp and bullheads. The last time Albert had
surfaced, a crowd that had gathered on the eastern
shore of the lake pelted him with rocks and pop
bottles. Assistant Zoo foreman Mike Kinsey was
worried: "People could hurt the poor guy throwing
things at him." Zoo officials had other worries as
well. Albert was in danger of becoming a handbag
if the wrong people succeeded in catching him. Or,
if he left the lake and wandered onto a heavily
traveled boulevard, he could be run over by a car
or truck. Albert was in real danger, but he didn't
know it.

Reading Psalm 121 recently, I was struck by
the phrase, "The Lord is thy keeper." What a blessed thought! God has committed himself to keep me
in all my ways as I abide under the shadow of the
Almighty (Psalm 91:1, 11). But, like Albert, I can
choose to leave this place of blessing and safety and
go off on my own in a life of independence, which is
to say a life of disobedience and rebellion. If I do
that, I'm in trouble. The world, the flesh, and the
devil may appear to offer free, fun-filled, and exciting experiences, but those of us who have tasted
the bitter fruits of disobedience know better. The
devil will promise a life that glitters with excitement
and success, but it is all a lie. The life of disciplined
obedience to the word of God is the only real path
to joy and freedom. I can escape from God, but it
will be to my own hurt and possible destruction.

Obedience as a way of life is the foundation upon which is built a lifetime of fruitful service, joyful fellowship with God and my brothers and sisters in Christ, guidance from God through his word, and a powerful prayer life.

The apostle John clearly links answered prayer to obedience. "And whatsoever we ask, we receive of him, because we keep his commandments, and do those things that are pleasing in his sight"(1 John 3:22). God will speak to us from his word when we are ready to listen to what God says and do what God commands. He will also answer our prayers when we are ready to obey him. In this passage the words "keep" and "do" are in the present tense; thus John teaches that obedience is *a way of life*. If we weigh each command from God to decide whether to go along with it or not, we cannot claim this promise. It is valid only for the person who has made a deep, bedrock commitment to live an obedient life which echoes the stirring declaration of the apostle Peter, "We must obey God." Instantly. Persistently. Not only when convenient. Not only when comfortable. Not only when prudent or logical. Regular, consistent answers to prayer depend on regular, consistent obedience. The obedient person's prayers are aimed at the honor and glory of God. They also contribute to that person's spiritual development.

The Old Testament insists that obedience is a

requirement for answers to prayer: "The sacrifice of the wicked is an abomination to the Lord: but the prayer of the upright is his delight. The way of the wicked is an abomination unto the Lord: but he loveth him that followeth after righteousness" (Proverbs 15:8–9).

Let me suggest a little exercise that could greatly enhance your power with God in prayer. The next time you pray, ask yourself, "Right now, at this moment, is my prayer an abomination to the Lord? Or is it a delight to him?" Pray the prayer of David: "Search me, O God, and know my heart: try me, and know my thoughts: And see if there be any wicked way in me, and lead me in the way everlasting" (Psalm 139:23–24).

David did not engage in the unproductive and defeating practice of introspection. He asked God to examine his life to show him if he was harboring unconfessed sin. Self-inspection is futile. When I try to examine myself I really do "see through a glass darkly." I miss things. I am prone to gloss over certain faults. I practice self-justification. But if God does the searching, it is different. His eye is sharp. His judgment is true. The window of my soul is transparent to his penetrating gaze.

And yet in light of all that, David is eager for God to search his life. He opens the windows of his life and lets the sin-destroying and life-giving breeze of the Holy Spirit blow through. He asks

God's help to find and destroy the sin that lurks within.

Such an open attitude is practically unknown in modern society. Cover-ups seem to be the norm. David, however, pleads with God to use any means necessary to get at the truth, no matter how painful. We are reminded of the words of Job, "Neither have I gone back from the commandment of his lips; I have esteemed the words of his mouth more than my necessary food" (Job 23:12). David calls for the all-knowing, gracious, loving God to probe around, to move from one chamber of his heart to another, to search out the wrong, cleanse it by his grace, and lead him into new surrender to the will of God. God's primary means of doing this is by his word. "For the word of God is quick, and powerful, and sharper than any two-edged sword, piercing even to the dividing asunder of soul and spirit, and of the joints and marrow, and is a discerner of the thoughts and intents of the heart" (Hebrews 4:12).

When I read David's prayer, I am reminded of a diligent, zealous, competent customs official I once saw examining a man's bags in the Moscow airport. The agent took the man's electric razor apart. He unrolled his socks. He felt the lining of his suitcase. He unfolded each tee shirt. He unscrewed the back off his alarm clock. And through it all the man whose bag was being inspected was agitated, nervous, and resentful. He didn't like it. In his prayer David took the exact opposite attitude. Had God been the customs agent, David would have been encouraging him to make a thorough search.

One of the problems in personalizing this great prayer of David is that it can be worn smooth by our familiarity with it. We've heard those words many times. We can quote them from memory. Those words, which vibrate with power to change our lives, can be so weakened through familiarity that they leave no mark on our consciences. To overcome this problem, the next time you pray this prayer, emphasize the words "search," "know," "try," "any," and "me." You will be doing two things: First, you will be asking the great physician to inspect your heart for any concealed disease. His diagnosis is necessary before he can heal you. Second, you will be admitting to the Lord that there are foes of his in your life that are so powerful that no one can overcome them but God himself.

The psalmist recognized the absolute necessity of obedience as a lifestyle if God is to answer prayer: "If I *regard* iniquity in my heart, the Lord will not hear me" (Psalm 66:18). Let me illustrate what it means to regard iniquity. I was wounded in a battle in the Pacific while serving with the Marines in World War II. I was sent to the Naval Hospital on Guadalcanal, and after treatment there was shipped, with other wounded Marines, to the Naval Hospital in Honolulu. When we arrived in Hawaii we could hardly wait for liberty so that we could hobble around downtown on our canes and crutches and experience a few of the pleasures of civilization again. The thing I craved was ice cream. Finally my day of freedom arrived. I left the hospital and made my way to an ice cream parlor. When the waitress asked what I wanted, I pointed to a large mixing bowl sitting on the shelf and told her to fill it up. She seemed startled, but she filled it. I sat down to eat that delicious ice cream I had craved and daydreamed about. I was in no hurry. I let each bite melt in my mouth. I rolled it around, under, and over my tongue, savoring each spoonful. I *loved* it. I *relished* it. It brought pleasure and gratified a hunger I had known for months. I basked in the sheer joy of the experience. That is what it means to regard iniquity in my heart. I treat it like a long lost friend. I treat it as a welcome guest in my home. I feed it with a fertile imagination and a lustful mind. The thought of parting with it brings me grief and anguish.

When I treat sin in that fashion, God will not hear my prayers. Obviously, to live a life in direct opposition to God and then to ask his help in doing it would be folly. When I thus fondle sin, it blocks access to God in prayer and also blocks the answer from God. God will not pay attention to my prayers while I am relishing my sin. We must remember, however, that though the world, the flesh, or the devil may gain a temporary victory in our lives, the situation is never hopeless. To a Christian who is awakened by the Spirit of God and who in humility and shame turns back to his Father, confessing and repenting of his sins, God grants a clean slate. The cleansed child of God can then pray with confidence. But until he makes such confession he cannot pray in the Spirit, in faith, or with fervency.

Often the person who is enjoying his sin instead of facing up to it will try to gain God's favor by doing something religious. The prophet Isaiah saw this tendency in Israel and spoke out against it.

> Hear the word of the Lord, ye rulers of Sodom; give ear unto the law of our God, ye people of Gomorrah. To what purpose is the multitude of your sacrifices unto me? saith the Lord: I am full of the burnt offerings of rams, and the fat of fed beasts; and I delight not in the blood of bullocks, or of lambs, or of he goats. When ye come to appear before me, who hath required this at your hand, to tread my courts? Bring no more vain oblations; incense is an abomination unto me; the new moons and sabbaths, the calling of assemblies, I cannot away with it; it is iniquity, even the solemn meeting. Your new moons and your appointed feasts my soul hateth: they are a

trouble unto me; I am weary to bear them. And when ye spread forth your hands, I will hide mine eyes from you: yea, when ye make many prayers, I will not hear: your hands are full of blood.

Wash you, make you clean; put away the evil of your doings from before mine eyes; cease to do evil; Learn to do well; seek judgment, relieve the oppressed, judge the fatherless, plead for the widow. Come now, and let us reason together, saith the Lord: though your sins be as scarlet, they shall be as white as snow; though they be red like crimson, they shall be as wool. If ye be willing and obedient, ye shall eat the good of the land: But if ye refuse and rebel, ye shall be devoured with the sword: for the mouth of the Lord hath spoken it. (Isaiah 1:10–20)

God's request of them was simple: let his word be their rule of life. But they had other plans. Rather than repent of sin and turn back to the Lord, they tried to win his favor through sacrifices, burnt offerings, and incense. They were eager to go through certain forms and rituals. They went to the right place at the right time to do the wrong thing. Their hearts were void of love for God and of obedience to his laws. They were more than willing to offer their sacrifices, but they would not give up their sins. All ritual, without obedience, is an affront to God. His word to them was, "Cease to do evil. Learn to do well. Come to me in obedience." But obedience was far from their thoughts. They wanted to keep their sin and bribe God with religious acts.

I know a young man who for years has been living in disobedience to God. Whenever I see him or talk with him on the phone, his conversation is filled with all the right words. He has been reading the book of James. Or he has been praying. Or he has been memorizing some verses. And on and on and on. He will do *anything*, it seems, except live a life of obedience to God. And he is miserable. He cries. He asks for our prayers. His life is a perfect photocopy of Jesus' story about the two foundations in Matthew 7:24–27.

There is a pathetic truth in this passage. The man who built his house on the sand worked just as hard as the man who built on the rock. They both hammered and sawed and painted and sweated in the midday sun. But for one it was all to no avail. He did not build on the right foundation. The wise man heard the sayings of Christ and obeyed them. The fool heard the same sayings and decided to ignore them. His life ended in ruin.

The Christian life must be a life of obedience. James minces no words: "But be ye doers of the word, and not hearers only, deceiving your own selves" (James 1:22). It is important to listen to

God's word. It is important to study the Scriptures. But if we stop there, we deceive ourselves. Jesus said, "Blessed are they that hear the word of God, *and keep it*" (Luke 11:28). The life of the young man I mentioned above proves the opposite truth as well: "Unhappy are those who hear the word of God and do not keep it." The apostle John sums up this truth: "Little children, let no man deceive you: he that *doeth* righteousness is righteous, even as he is righteous" (1 John 3:7).

Recently I visited a Sunday school classroom where small children meet. On the wall was a piece of paper with the words "Rules from God" at the top. There were five rules:

1. Don't talk.
2. No fighting.
3. Don't change the subject.
4. No goofing around.
5. Obey.

As I read them I knew there was an experienced teacher who led that class. She had probably been at it for years and knew the problems. She stated the rules in very specific terms.

What does Jesus mean by "hear" and "do"? The answer is both negative and positive. We must determine to abstain from the things he forbids, and we must do those that he commands. When what he wants us to do is clear to us, we must not hesitate to obey.

In the summer of 1980 I spent four months with my wife on a preaching tour of Europe. We spent the month of June in England. Part of that time was spent with a longtime friend. One afternoon we observed Parliament in session. For an American it is an awesome thing to walk those historic halls, to sit in the magnificent rotunda, to view the majesty and splendor that is a part of British history. My wife and I felt out of place. We were on our best behavior—trying not to do anything that would offend. We mentioned this eagerness to conform later to our British friend, and he told us about something that had happened to one group of American tourists who had visited the halls of Parliament. These forty Americans in their orange walking shorts, green tennis shoes, and flowered shirts were walking together in a group when they were confronted by Lord Hailsham, a member of the House of Lords. He is an awesome figure in his splendid robe and wig. At that moment Lord Hailsham saw across the hall Mr. Neil Kennock, an M.P. in the Labor Party with whom he had some urgent business. He tried to catch Kennock's eye, but to no avail; the tourists were between the two men. After several futile attempts Lord Hailsham called out in desperation over the heads of the Americans in a great booming voice, "Neil!" And all forty of them did!

When my friend told the story he roared with

laughter. The thought of those forty Americans on their knees on that marble floor was a hilarious picture in his mind. But Virginia and I didn't laugh. We knew that had we been among them we would have been the first to kneel. To me, that is an illustration of the kind of obedience God wants from us. When he commands, we obey—instantly.

Jesus is our best example of obedience. Remember his word to his disciples, "My meat is to do the will of him that sent me, and to finish his work" (John 4:34). In the Garden of Gethsemane, after expressing his total revulsion at the humiliation and infinite agony of the crucifixion, Jesus said to the Father, "Nevertheless, not my will, but thine be done." He did the thing that his soul hated most—"he became sin for us"—because it was his Father's will. Singlemindedly, throughout the gospel of John, Jesus Christ pressed ahead doing his Father's will.

If you and I want to serve God effectively, have fellowship with him in Spirit and truth, and see answers to our prayers, we too must obey him. "The eyes of the Lord are upon the righteous, and his ears are open unto their cry"(Psalm 34:15). The blind man whose eyes Jesus opened summarized this crucial truth: "if any man be a worshipper of God, *and doeth his will*, him he heareth" (John 9:31).

5
Humility

HE FORGETTETH NOT
THE CRY OF THE HUMBLE.

Psalm 9:12

IT WOULD HAVE been hard to find two men more different from each other. One perceived himself as a very good man. The other was ashamed of himself. One was admired by the religious people when he walked down the street. The other was hated. One was looked upon as the essence of God-fearing respectability. The other was a crook. It is these things that make the ending of the story about these two men such a shocker. It is one of

Jesus' most fascinating parables. In order to make sure his audience got the point, Jesus explained the moral of the story at both the beginning and the end:

> And he spake this parable unto certain which trusted in themselves that they were righteous, and despised others: Two men went up into the temple to pray; the one a Pharisee, and the other a publican. The Pharisee stood and prayed thus with himself, God, I thank thee, that I am not as other men are, extortioners, unjust, adulterers, or even as this publican. I fast twice in the week, I give tithes of all that I possess. And the publican, standing afar off, would not lift up so much as his eyes unto heaven, but smote upon his breast, saying, God be merciful to me a sinner. I tell you, this man went down to his house justified rather than the other: for every one that exalteth himself shall be abased; and he that humbleth himself shall be exalted. (Luke 18:9–14)

Jesus directs his message here at those self-righteous people who hold others in contempt. Apparently, the Pharisee's main interest was to make a good impression. He hoped that he would be in the spotlight—with every eye on him as he strutted up to God's house. The applause of men meant more to him than the approval of God. Jesus was talking about people like him when he said, "all their works they do for to be seen of men" (Matthew 23:5), and "for a pretense [they] make long prayers" (Mark 12:40). The Pharisee was self-centered, not God-centered.

Anyone who has been kept from gross sins *should* thank the Lord. But this man didn't stop there. His pride led him to cut himself off from the rest of humanity and to declare himself "holier than thou." As he was congratulating himself, his contemptuous eye fell on the sinful publican, whom he used as an example of all the ugly things that he was not. He stopped reciting the things he didn't do, and began to brag about those things he did. He fasted and tithed. Listening to his prayer we realize that he felt no need to confess any sins or to cry out to God to supply physical or spiritual need. He had everything. He had arrived. It was not his actions, however, but his attitude that Jesus criticized. His religious performance was faultless, but his contemptuous and haughty spirit was sinful. His good works became a stench in the nostrils of God.

It is interesting to note that in his zeal to impress all those around him, the Pharisee completely lost sight of his objective. He had gone up into the temple to pray. But he was so taken up with his own goodness that all he did was go to a conspicuous place and recite his own virtues—aloud!

Now look at the publican. What a contrast! In

his own eyes he was the greatest of sinners, so he quietly crept over to a corner where he earnestly pled for mercy. He probably did not realize he was touching God's heart, but the Lord makes it clear that his heart is touched by the humble and penitent sinner: "The Lord is nigh unto them that are of a broken heart; and saveth such as be of a contrite spirit" (Psalm 34:18). This passage is tremendously encouraging to those of us who realize our need for forgiveness and grace.

Then comes the surprise—it is the *publican* who is justified in the sight of God. Why not the Pharisee? Simple. He saw no need to receive the righteousness of God. He had already pronounced *himself* righteous. His haughty attitude prevented him from true communion with the One who "resists the proud but gives grace to the humble" (James 4:6).

There are some things that cannot be mixed: oil and water, pride and humility. A quick review of a few passages will immediately show why. Jesus referred to himself as "meek and *lowly* in heart" (Matthew 11:29). The word *humble* in the New Testament always comes across like that. Phrases such as "of *low* degree," "brought *low*," and "*lowly*" are used to describe the humble person. But the word *pride* goes in the opposite direction: "lifted *up* with pride," "puffed *up*," "*high* minded." Humility leads one lower; pride leads one higher.

In the upper room Jesus became a servant: "Jesus, knowing that the Father had given all things into his hands, and that he was come from God, and went to God; He riseth from supper, and laid aside his garments; and took a towel, and girded himself. After that he poureth the water into a basin, and began to wash the disciples' feet" (John 13:3-5). This scene answers some of the most profound questions ever asked. What is God like? Look at Christ in the upper room. He stooped to serve man. What should man be like? Look at Christ in the upper room. We too should be servants. You do not need a stepladder to wash a person's feet. You don't go *up*, you kneel *down*.

But the joy of being a humble servant is often poisoned by pride. If we are asked to do a lowly task, we rebel against it. We are quick to declare, "that's not part of my job description," or "I'm better than you; you do it." What a pity! So many kind and helpful things go undone because we think that to do them would indicate inferiority on our part. We rob ourselves of the privilege of doing Christ-like service by heeding the whispered insinuations of the devil.

We are all infected with the craving to climb socially. Name-dropping is a subtle effort to climb. "Last week I got a call from ———." "I was at a party chatting with ———." "Yesterday at church ——— came over and asked my opinion about what the class should study next." Name-dropping is not our only means of exalting ourselves. "Oh, you like that painting? I picked it up the last time I was in Milan." "Our house is the one up on the hill overlooking all the rest." If any of these examples strike a familiar chord, think for a moment on Proverbs 30:32: "If thou has done foolishly in lifting up thyself, or if thou hast thought evil, lay thine hand upon thy mouth."

Acting proudly and speaking proudly are foolish. Why? Because the result is usually the opposite of what you are seeking.

Recently my son and I were shopping for a camera. As is our custom when shopping, we visited a half-dozen stores before making up our minds to go ahead with the purchase. We ruled out two of the stores simply because of the salesmen's attitudes. They weren't exactly rude; but they were haughty, and therefore obnoxious. They knew everything about everything, but it seemed painful and distasteful to have to explain things to someone as ignorant as I am. Their prices weren't any higher than at other stores; in fact one of them had a nice camera on sale. But their attitudes killed our desire to buy.

My son also wanted to buy an engraved wedding band for his fiance. We went into a local jeweler's, and he explained that he wanted a Bible reference—1 John 4:7—engraved on the inside of the band. The lady who waited on us was very helpful. As we left the store, my son said the reason he bought the band at that store was because the owners acted just like ordinary people. He had shopped at some stores where the people seemed arrogant. Their attitude turned him off. We all like people who don't "lift up themselves" above us but treat us as equals.

Some months ago I listened to some friends telling me about their house guest. A very important person was staying in their home for a few days. But my friends had a problem: the fact that Mr. Big was stopping in their home had gone to their heads. It had become something to brag about. Their pride was showing. As I listened, the thought crossed my mind, What if truly famous persons, such as the Prince and Princess of Wales or the President of the United States, were to visit them? They would probably explode with pride!

Isaiah 57:15 reveals God's values: "For thus saith the high and lofty One that inhabiteth eternity, whose name is Holy; I dwell in the high and holy place, with him also that is of a contrite and humble spirit, to revive the spirit of the humble, and to revive the heart of the contrite ones." Remember the words of Jesus: "Whosoever therefore shall humble himself as this little child, the same is greatest in the kingdom of heaven" (Matthew 18:4).

A humble spirit and a powerful prayer life go hand in hand. "Lord, thou hast heard the desire of the humble: thou wilt prepare their heart, thou wilt cause thine ear to hear" (Psalm 10:17). God delights to fill the life of the humble with good things. God is unable to fill a life that is already full of arrogance and pride. But "he forgetteth not the cry of the humble" (Psalm 9:12).

Overseas care packages are stamped with the reminder, "A gift from the people of the United States." As you and I reflect on our lives as Christians, there are hundreds of blessings that have come into our lives whose origin is God himself. They would have to be stamped "obtained by God's grace—through humble heartfelt prayer." Humility is the realization that his strength is made perfect in our weakness.

Prayer is a powerful weapon in our struggle against Satan. Scripture calls Satan a dragon, a snake, and a lion. These images reflect his hatred, cleverness, and power. But his power is overcome as the Christian humbles himself before God. The screams of the dragon, the hiss of the serpent, and the roar of the lion cannot drown out the quiet pleading of the humble heart.

Prayer is a haven in the storm, an anchor for the soul being buffeted by the waves of fear and doubt, a shepherd's staff to the one ready to fall, a chest of priceless jewels to the poor in spirit. The prayer of the arrogant goes unheeded, but "he forgetteth not the cry of the humble."

Jesus told his disciples that he was "meek and lowly in heart." Humility, therefore, is a Christlike attribute. It is little wonder, then, that the meek and lowly have a special place in the heart of God. They remind him of his Son, who voluntarily "humbled himself, and became obedient unto death, even the death of the cross" (Philippians 2:8). We are not surprised, then, when we read, "The meek will he guide in judgment: and the meek will he teach his way" (Psalm 25:9). The meek and lowly are not puffed up with their own resources, their own abilities, their own wisdom. The truly humble people of this world fully realize their dependence on God. He promises to reward their dependence on him.

People in positions of leadership are particularly susceptible to the sin of pride. Their gifts are often more public; they are more motivated; and they tend to have a greater understanding of the overall mission than the followers. For that reason I have often suggested to young men in training for leadership positions that they study 2 Chronicles 26, the chapter that tells the story of the reign of Uzziah. As a young man this king demonstrated deep devotion to the Lord: "He sought God in the days of Zechariah" (verse 5). When God spoke, he obeyed: "He did that which was right in the sight of the Lord" (4). Is it any wonder that God blessed his life? "As long as he sought the Lord, God made him to prosper" (5). God helped him against his foes. His fame was spread abroad. He was diligent to see to the security, protection, and well-being of his people (see verses 9–15). He loved the land. Farming was in his blood. He was a wonderful leader, and the people expected him to have a long and happy life under the favor of God.

None of the things that brought other great men down were found in Uzziah's life. The gross sins of immorality, murder, or idolatry did not plague him. But there was one sin that ruined his life. It hit with the devastation of an earthquake. "His heart was lifted up to his destruction" (verse 16). Pride led him to become an outcast from his people and a stranger to the altar of God. He was ruined.

This is truly an amazing tale. There were kings who practiced the great sins of oppression or immorality or murder; yet they were restored to the favor of God. But Uzziah's pride led him down a road of sorrow and regret. His humble heart had brought him blessing, but his pride ruined him.

Let me close this chapter by asking you a question. What do the following people have in common: Mary, the Mother of Jesus (Luke 1:38), Abraham (Genesis 18:27), Moses (Exodus 3:11), David (2 Samuel 7:18), Solomon (1 Kings 3:7),

Asaph (Psalm 73:22), Agur (Proverbs 30:2), Isaiah (Isaiah 6:5), Jeremiah (Jeremiah 1:6), Daniel (Daniel 2:30), John the Baptist (John 1:27), the centurion with the sick servant (Matthew 8:8), Paul (Ephesians 3:8), and the twenty-four elders of Revelation (4:10)? If your answer to the question is humility, you are right. Humility has been called "the queen of all virtues." It is no accident that these men and women were marked out by God as great in his kingdom. Their lives were filled with humble gratitude, humble dependence, and humble adoration and praise. "By humility and the fear of the Lord are riches, and honour, and life" (Proverbs 22:4).

6
Faith

AND ALL THINGS, WHATSOEVER
YE SHALL ASK IN PRAYER, BELIEVING,
YE SHALL RECEIVE.

Matthew 21:22

THE LIGHTNING FLASHED as our plane bounced along in the midnight storm. I had been in airplanes in bad storms before, but this was different. We were over the heart of the Amazon jungle, a wild and dangerous part of the world. If we did go down, and if by some miracle we survived the crash, we probably wouldn't last long. I reflected on the fate of the boat-load of people who had perished in the jungle just the week before. An overloaded triple-decker river boat had capsized and sunk in the Amazon River. More than three hundred were feared dead. The captain was arrested and imprisoned for negligence. Many of the survivors had warned him that his boat was leaking, but he had told them to mind their own business. He assured them the boat was safe. But now there were hundreds of people dead in the Amazon river, many of them eaten by *candriv*, a small piranha-like fish, thinner than a piranha but much more voracious. As I sat there on the bouncing, shuddering, jerking plane, I was thankful that the pilot of our airplane, unlike the riverboat captain, was a highly competent, trustworthy man who could be relied upon.

Like the Amazon jungle, our world is a dangerous place. Terrorists roam the globe killing wantonly and holding innocent people hostage. Disease and accidents claim the lives of thousands. Thieves infest our streets.

In the spiritual realm the devil walks about as a roaring lion seeking whom he may devour. As we launch out on the sea of life, it is a blessing to know we have a trustworthy Pilot at the helm in whom we can confidently place our faith, knowing he will never fail us nor forsake us.

In his great hymn, "Jesus, Savior, Pilot Me," Edward Hopper declares that Christ is a trustworthy pilot of our small craft:

Jesus Savior, pilot me
Over life's tempestuous sea.
Unknown waves before me roll,
Hiding rocks and treacherous shoal.
Chart and compass come from thee;
Jesus, Savior, pilot me.

A few weeks ago I attended the funeral of one of our close associates in Curitiba, Brazil. Mario, a young man of thirty-two, had died of cancer. He had known Christ as his Savior for about six years. The night before the funeral Ken and Carol Lottis, the Navigator representatives, and my wife Virginia and I went to the chapel where Mario's wife, Betty, and some other friends had gathered. In the room next door another group of people had gathered to mourn the loss of one of their own. The contrast between the two groups was vivid. In the room next door, they were wailing in anguish. One lady collapsed. There was fear and desperation in the sounds from that room. Although Betty and her friends were sad, they did not agonize like those next door who had no hope. There was sorrow, but there was also peace, assurance, and a hope based on the word of Christ: "In my Father's house are many mansions: if it were not so, I would have told you. I go to prepare a place for you. And if I go and prepare a place for you, I will come again, and receive you unto myself; that where I am, there ye may be also" (John 14:2–3). Jesus Christ was taking them through the rough waters of separation and sorrow, giving them victory. The third stanza of Edward Hopper's hymn restates his confidence in his Pilot.

> When at last I near the shore,
> And the fearful breakers roar
> Twixt me and the peaceful rest;
> Then while leaning on Thy breast,
> May I hear Thee say to me,
> "Fear not, I will pilot thee."

There is no area in the Christian life in which faith plays a more important role than prayer. Faith in Jesus Christ is the bedrock upon which a solid prayer life is built. Matthew 21:22 clearly shows the tie between faith and prayer: "And all things whatsoever ye shall ask in prayer, believing, ye shall receive." The context of Jesus' promise is the incident of the barren fig tree:

> Now in the morning as he returned into the city, he hungered. And when he saw a fig tree in the way, he came to it, and found nothing thereon, but leaves only, and said unto it, Let no fruit grow on thee henceforward forever. And presently the fig tree withered away. And when the disciples saw it, they marvelled, saying, How soon is the fig tree withered away! Jesus

answered and said unto them, Verily I say unto you, If ye have faith, and doubt not, ye shall not only do this which is done to the fig tree, but also if ye shall say unto this mountain, Be thou removed, and be thou cast into the sea; it shall be done. (Matthew 21:18–21)

Note carefully the phrase, "if ye have faith, and doubt not." When we doubt the goodness, the grace, the power, and the presence of God, we nullify the prayer of faith. It is the prayer of faith that triggers the promise of God. God's power is always available, but he waits for the catalyst of prayer to activate it in our behalf.

A local newscaster recently told of two families who were going to drive from Colorado Springs to Michigan in their campers. As they were getting the campers ready for the trip, one of the men struck a match to light the gas water heater. There was a tremendous explosion. The side of the camper (in many parts of the world these are called caravans) was blown out. Fortunately, no one was injured badly.

The rescue squad discovered that the gas line had somehow been hooked up improperly, and gas was escaping into the room. When the match was struck, the gas exploded. All of that latent power was in the room, but the match was the catalyst that set it off.

That is a picture of the relationship between the activity of God and the prayer of faith. The blessings of God are there, waiting to be activated when we pray.

The promises of Jesus cannot fail. Therefore we can come to the throne of grace in confidence. But we must "ask in prayer, *believing*" (Matthew 21:22). Then no obstacle—not even a mountain—can stand before the power of our confident faith in God *and the answer to prayer that springs from that faith*. How can that be?

The answer lies in the fact that this kind of faith has its roots in God's revealed word. Faith to move a mountain can be exercised only when we are sure that God has told us to remove one. At this point in the training of the twelve our Lord seemed to be trying to instill into his disciples the excitement of the assurance that God answers prayer and that his power was available to them. He wanted to help them become men who prayed and walked by faith. He wants to teach you and me the same lesson.

Two years ago my wife and I decided to leave our townhouse in Colorado Springs and move to a home nearer The Navigators' headquarters at Glen Eyrie, where I had my office. We arranged for some help from the work crew at the Glen, and our son recruited a few fellows and girls from his college friends at the church. Moving day arrived with a threatening sky. There were clouds over Pikes Peak and lightning in the west. The weatherman predicted a rainy day.

My heart sank. Moving in an open truck on a rainy day is not my idea of a good time. I began to complain and fret. My son Randy heard me, walked over, put his hand on my shoulder, and said, "Cheer up, Dad. It's not going to rain. We prayed, didn't we?" His faith inspired me. I cheered up. We rolled up our sleeves and went to work. The lightning flashed. The wind blew. The thunder rolled. And we didn't get a sprinkle!

God continues to help me learn to trust him. Faith doesn't come easily, but as we read the record, we discover that trust didn't come easily to the apostles either. But they kept following, trusting, growing, and praying. We must follow their example. His word to us is unequivocal: "Therefore I say unto you, What things soever ye desire, when ye pray, believe that ye receive them, and ye shall have them" (Mark 11:24).

James emphasizes the link between prayer and faith: "But let him ask in faith, nothing wavering. For he that wavereth is like a wave of the sea driven with the wind and tossed. For let not that man think that he shall receive any thing of the Lord. A double minded man is unstable in all his ways" (James 1:6–8). Our faith must not stagger at circumstances. If we fix our eyes on difficulties and trials, we will be filled with doubts and feel defeated. But if we fix our eyes on God and set our faith on him, he will bring us security and stability.

Abraham, the father of faith, is a prime example of this kind of faith:

> Who against hope believed in hope, that he might become the father of many nations, according to that which was spoken, So shall thy seed be. And being not weak in faith, he considered not his own body now dead, when he was about an hundred years old, neither yet the deadness of Sarah's womb. He staggered not at the promise of God through unbelief; but was strong in faith, giving glory to God; and being fully persuaded that, what he had promised, he was able also to perform. (Romans 4:18–21)

Here was a man who knew God. He believed in his creative power. He believed God could raise the dead. With those facts firmly fixed in his mind he could maintain hope even when all cause for human hope was gone.

To Abraham the promises of God had more authority than logic, science, or history. God's promise was believable in spite of impossible circumstances.

You and I have an enemy who will do everything in his power to keep us from this kind of faith. The primary focus of his attack is always the Bible.

He will tell us it is culturally irrelevant, that its words are for a different time, or that human error has nullified its reliability.

For millions around the world who have no Bible, his attacks take a different form. Voodoo, for example, is a form of Satanic activity. While in Brazil recently, I was surprised to see the use of the hex so widespread. Spirit worship is rampant. By day men and women conduct business as usual. They work in modern offices and drive modern cars. They wear well-tailored business suits. They live in comfortable, clean homes. They eat well, live well, and enjoy all the comforts of modern civilization. But at night a change over them. The men can be found creeping through the streets carrying candles, birds, flowers, or grain. They light the candles and arrange them around some grain or flowers (depending on whether the demon prefers food or something pretty), kill the bird, and chant the appropriate curse on their enemy who lives nearby.

In another part of the world the devil deludes millions of people into trying to experience God's forgiveness through washing in a holy river. From sunrise to sunset thousands of people bathe in this river, draw their drinking water from it, and bury their dead in its depths. Nearby, priests conduct their Satan-inspired rites in a temple containing thousands of rats which they believe to be reincarnated people. They feed them and provide huge buckets of water from which the rats can drink. The pagan deity that inspires all of this idolatry is worshiped with an unholy zeal. As we reflect on the worship of the pagan world with its hideous rites and practices, we can rejoice that we know the God of Abraham who speaks his promises to us in his word. Like Abraham, we are called upon to believe these promises.

The record does not state, however, that Abraham had no inward struggle with doubt. It only tells us that his faith triumphed. Our hearts will never be so devoted, our wills so disciplined, or our minds so enlightened that we will not entertain a shade of doubt. We will always find our new nature in conflict with the weakness of our fallen humanity. At times we can be greatly troubled, violently shaken, and under great stress, but through faith we can triumph.

It is that sort of tested faith upon which our life of prayer is built. God does not hear and answer our prayer because we are worthy. God does not dole out his grace, his pardon, his love, or his mercy in response to our goodness, but in response to *our need* which prompts our cry of dependence and our prayer of faith. Remember Abraham. Even though the situation seemed absolutely hopeless, Abraham became fully persuaded that what God had promised he was able also to perform.

The writer of the book of Hebrews encourages us to exercise this same "holy persuasion":

> Having therefore, brethren, boldness to enter into the holiest by the blood of Jesus, By a new and living way, which he hath consecrated for us, through the veil, that is to say, his flesh; and having an high priest over the house of God; Let us draw near with a true heart in full assurance of faith, having our hearts sprinkled from an evil conscience, and our bodies washed with pure water. Let us hold fast the profession of our faith without wavering; (for he is faithful that promised). (Hebrews 10:19–23)

An active life of faith sends us to our knees to pray with boldness. Nothing now blocks our way into the holy of holies. We have free access to the throne of grace by the blood of Christ. But we need to remind people of this fact.

On a recent overseas preaching tour I was warned about the unethical practices of the passport control officials of a certain country. Our passports were up to date. We had visas. Getting into the country was no problem. The problem was getting out. If we told them we were going to be in the country ten days they would mark our stay for five days. Then ten days later, when it came time to leave, they would point out that we were in the country illegally, because we were there five days longer than we had stated. No amount of arguing would do any good. It was simply a matter of their demanding a few dollars in bribe money to let us past the desk and give us access to our airplane. All of this caused us a great deal of uncertainty over whether we would have trouble getting out this time.

The attitude of uneasiness that these officials created in me reminded me, by contrast, of the confidence we have in God. We never feel this way at the throne of grace. We can draw near in full assurance of faith, remembering that he is faithful who promised. Our faith is based on the faithfulness of God.

Can you recall any statement by the Lord Jesus in which he rebuked his followers for expecting too much of him? For asking too much? For thinking too highly of him? No. His rebuke was for not expecting enough. Do you recall the day he and three of his followers came down from the mount and found his disciples helpless before the power of an evil spirit? Look at the record:

> And when he came to his disciples, he saw a
> great multitude about them, and the scribes
> questioning with them. And straightway all the
> people, when they beheld him, were greatly
> amazed, and running to him saluted him. And
> he asked the scribes, What question ye with

them? And one of the multitude answered and
said, Master, I have brought unto thee my son,
which hath a dumb spirit; And wheresoever he
taketh him, he teareth him: and he foameth, and
gnasheth with his teeth, and pineth away: and I
spake to thy disciples that they should cast him
out; and they could not. He answereth him, and
saith, O faithless generation, how long shall I be
with you? how long shall I suffer you? bring him
unto me. And they brought him unto him: and
when he saw him, straightway the spirit tare
him; and he fell on the ground, and wallowed
foaming. And he asked his father, How long is it
ago since this came unto him? And he said, Of a
child. And oftimes it hath cast him into the fire,
and into the waters, to destroy him: but if thou
canst do any thing, have compassion on us, and
help us. Jesus said unto him, If thou canst
believe, all things are possible to him that
believeth. And straightway the father of the
child cried out, and said with tears, Lord, I
believe; help thou mine unbelief. When Jesus
saw that the people came running together, he
rebuked the foul spirit, saying unto him, Thou
dumb and deaf spirit, I charge thee, come out of
him, and enter no more into him. And the spirit
cried, and rent him sore, and came out of him:
and he was as one dead; insomuch that many
said, He is dead. But Jesus took him by the hand,

and lifted him up; and he arose. And when he was come into the house, his disciples asked him privately, Why could not we cast him out? And he said unto them, This kind can come forth by nothing, but by prayer and fasting. (Mark 9:14–29)

Note carefully Jesus' words in verse nineteen. He did not exclaim "Oh bungling generation!" or "Oh powerless generation!" or "Oh inept generation!" He said, "Oh *faithless* generation!" And later, his words to the father of the boy were simple and direct: "If thou canst believe." He seems to be saying that his action depended on the father's believing. When the father saw that the whole matter waited for the birth of faith in his anguished struggling soul, he cried out with words that are a comfort to us all. He did not try to conceal the unbelief that still gripped him; he admitted the struggles of his heart. But even though he wrestled with unbelief, he shouted his faith: "Lord, I believe!" At the same time he cried out for deliverance from the distrust that still remained. His unbelief was not an obstinate, stiff-necked refusal to place his faith in Christ. Rather it was a weakness which he knew he could not overcome in his own strength. So he did a very wise thing—he called out to Christ for help.

There is an interesting contrast in this story.

Jesus seems to be quite tender and understanding with the father of the boy, but quite stern with his apostles. Why is this? I believe it goes back to the fact that he had given them the command to "cast out devils" and the power to do it. They had not been appropriating his power or obeying his command, because of the entrenched unbelief of the people. "And he did not many mighty works there because of their unbelief" (Matthew 13:58). Does he sorrowfully say the same thing today about our homes and churches? Is our ministry handcuffed because of unbelief?

According to Paul, there is no limit to what God can do. Paul stretches the limits of language to stir us into offering prayer commensurate with God's power: "Now unto him that is able to do exceeding abundantly above all that we ask or think, according to the power that worketh in us" (Ephesians 3:20). Note the phrase "exceeding abundantly above." The problem is never with God; the problem is in the scope of our thinking, obeying, and asking. The power and grace of God are inexhaustible. Our prayers can never drain dry the ocean of God's sufficiency. God is able to do far more than anything we can think about or pray about. Abundantly more. Exceeding abundantly more. So much more that it cannot be expressed in words.

7
A Burdened Heart

HE WEPT, AND MADE
SUPPLICATION UNTO HIM.

Hosea 12:4

WE WERE DESPERATE. We knew the crowd our daughter had begun to run with would lead her down the path of ruin. She had taken a job as a waitress in a pizza parlor, and some of the gang that worked with her were into drugs, booze, and wild parties. She was enamored of them—found them exciting. She had begun to stay out late, and when we asked about it she was quite frank with us. She liked this crowd. They were fun. She didn't see why we were concerned. It was really no big deal.

But we had a problem. We had seen our oldest son get involved with that same sort of crowd a few years earlier and had watched the difficulties that had come his way; and we certainly didn't want to see our daughter go that same route and experience those same troubles. So we talked about it with her, but it didn't do any good. Her general attitude was, "Oh, dad! It's okay. Don't worry." But we did worry. And nothing we said or did seemed to do any good. We were deeply burdened for Becky.

One day I suggested to my wife that we leave the house for a while and go somewhere to pray. We got into the car and drove to a quiet street, parked under a shade tree, and began to pray. We unburdened our hearts to God on behalf of our daughter. I have no idea how long we stayed there, but we were in no hurry. We were two parents with heavy hearts. Two parents with a deep concern. Two parents who knew of only one place to turn: the throne of grace where we might cast our burden upon the Lord.

After a long session of fervent prayer we returned home. Our daughter was at work and didn't get home until late that night. The next morning she dropped a bombshell. The girl who was the ringleader was leaving town and wanted Becky to go with her. "Are you going to go?" I asked. "No," she said, "I don't want to go away with her. That would be a dumb idea." That very day the girl left town, the gang broke up, and Becky lost interest in that way of life. The problem dissolved before our eyes. Becky was delivered from a situation that could have been her ruin. And it happened overnight. I am convinced it happened as a direct result of the fervent prayers of two burdened parents who pled with God for the deliverance of their daughter.

There are many passages in the Bible that describe fervent prayer. One of the clearest is the statement of James, "The effectual fervent prayer of a righteous man availeth much" (5:16). In this passage, and in others, we see that effective prayers burst forth from a burdened heart.

One of the first examples of fervent prayer in the Bible is Abraham pleading with God not to destroy Sodom. The sin of the twin cities was very grievous. Abraham certainly didn't approve of their vile practices. But he drew near to God and began to pour out his heart. I have heard preachers chuckle when they preached on the passage, regarding it as the story of a clever old Jew bargaining with God. But that is not the spirit of the passage. This is the picture of a man on his knees crying out from the depths of his heart.

Abraham's prayer was in response to the word of God, which told him what God was about to do. Abraham would never have prayed had God not spoken to him. It is like this with us. We decry our powerless and ineffectual prayers, not realizing that prayers with power come from people who are in daily communion with God. And communion with God is a two-way street. We respond in obedience as God speaks to us through his word, and he responds in faithfulness to us as we pour out our burdened hearts to him in prayer. God had spoken to Abraham about the city of Sodom, and Abraham responded by pleading on behalf of the people of Sodom.

This is an amazing story. Here was a man who was no doubt sickened by the sin of Sodom, but he was praying for its salvation rather than rejoicing in its misfortune.

I recently had an experience that revealed to me how far I am from this godly spirit. A friend of mine moved to Colorado Springs and bought a house. The house was occupied by four young men who agreed to be out by a certain date. On the day of the move my wife and I, our son Randy, and two other men went to the place to help my friend move in. To our utter amazement the young men who were supposed to be out were still in the house, fast asleep, with all of their possessions still there. So we made an agreement with them. We would move all of their stuff out, stack it in the yard, clean the house, then move all of Bob's stuff in. Two moves! When I heard what we had to do, I was bent out of shape. Whenever my wife and I moved from a place, we were always out on time, and we always left the house clean as a whistle. But here we were—emptying rooms, cleaning the rooms, and *then* moving in. And to top it off, the place was a pig pen. The house was not only filthy, but contained empty liquor bottles strewn about and the remains of marijuana parties.

So we began. Finally we got the stuff moved outside to the yard and the place cleaned; then we began to unload the truck and haul Bob's things into the house. And guess what! It began to rain, all over those guys' possessions—their fancy stereo gear, clothes, and household goods we had hauled out of the house and set in the yard. And guess what my reaction was. Did I follow Abraham's example and feel compassion for them? I did not. I was actually pleased to see their misfortune. "It serves them right," I thought. "Had they done what they were supposed to, it would never have happened." How unlike Abraham! How unlike Jeremiah, who, when confronted by the sins of the people, cried out, "My eyes fail from weeping. I am in torment within, my heart is poured out on the ground because my people are destroyed, because children and infants faint in the streets of the city" (Lamentations 2:11, NIV). How unlike Jesus, who wept over Jerusalem.

Abraham had a burdened heart. No doubt

part of his concern was for his nephew Lot, who lived in Sodom. Abraham had once demonstrated his concern for Lot by delivering him from his captors. Later, to avoid controversy, he let Lot have the choicest grazing land. Now he prayed in an effort to deliver him again. Lot's shabby treatment of Abraham in earlier years had long since been forgotten and forgiven, and Abraham was burdened for this ungrateful nephew.

The challenge of Abraham's heartfelt prayer can intimidate us. How could we ever be like that? Is it possible for us to actually follow the admonition of Jesus to "pray for those who despitefully use us"? How can we gain that sort of spirit? Jeremiah 30:21 offers a clue: "'I will bring him near and he will come close to me, for who is he who will devote himself to be close to me?' declares the Lord" (NIV). As we devote ourselves to being close to God he will help us have a burden for others. It has to come from the Lord, because a burden for others is contrary to human nature. A burdened heart leading to fervent prayer is the result of the Holy Spirit at work in our lives. Abraham recognized his weakness: "Behold now, I have taken upon me to speak unto the Lord, which am but dust and ashes" (Genesis 18:27). Fervent prayer is prompted by a realization that we are unworthy to approach the living God, that we are helpless, and that we depend on God absolutely.

Samuel was burdened to pray for a people who did not deserve it. The people had rejected Samuel's leadership and demanded a king. But when they found themselves in trouble they turned again to Samuel and asked for his prayers. "Pray for thy servants unto the Lord thy God, that we die not: for we have added unto all our sins this evil, to ask us a king" (1 Samuel 12:19).

Now think abut this situation for a minute. What would have been a very human response to that request? Suppose you have been treated very shabbily by a person—rejected and spurned. Then, to your amazement, that person comes to you and asks you for a favor—a *big* favor—something that requires a lot of time, energy, and hard work. Do you think you would be inclined to respond in a wholehearted and positive manner? Probably not. It would have been natural for Samuel to have said, "So! You want prayer, do you? Why don't you go to Saul and get *him* to pray for you? Why come running to me? I thought you didn't want me any more. Saul's your man—get him to pray for you."

But Samuel did not respond this way. Look at his remarkable answer: "Moreover as for me, God forbid that I should sin against the Lord in ceasing to pray for you: but I will teach you the good and the right way" (1 Samuel 12:23). In effect he is saying, "Pray for you? Of course I'll pray for you. Not to bear you up in prayer would be to neglect my responsibilities and to sin against God." Even as I put these words on paper, I'm struck with how strange they sound in our day.

Christian, God has commanded us to call upon him. But if we call *only* out of duty, our prayers will not be effectual; they will lack the vital ingredient of sincerity. When prayer becomes a habit, a duty, or a form, it has lost its power. Prayer must come from the heart. We have a responsibility to maintain daily communion with God, to plead with him to touch our hearts, so that we may offer our prayers in the right spirit.

David gives us the key to heartfelt prayer: "The Lord is nigh unto all them that call upon him, to all that call upon him in truth" (Psalm 145:18). The words "in truth" are crucial. A burdened heart speaks truly. A broken, crushed pleading soul does not fill his prayers with cold formality or pompous hypocrisy. A humble heart is not filled with the falsehood of pride. And this verse contains a great word which encompasses a great promise. The word is "all." *All* them that call upon him in truth. It is important for us to remember this word, so that we do not get caught in the trap of thinking that God plays favorites. We can read of men like Luther, Knox, and Praying Hyde and conclude that it is no use for "little old me" to approach the throne of grace and expect answers. This is the devil's lie. He uses this ploy to keep the people of God off their knees. No, the Lord is nigh to *"all"* who pour out their hearts to him in truth.

Human nature can also cloud our realization of God's eagerness to hear our prayers and answer them. Because we get impatient with others, we tend to think that God will get impatient with us. I recently played Ping-Pong with a five-year-old boy. He had never seen a Ping-Pong table before, never held a paddle and never hit a ball. He was full of questions. How do you score a point? What is the net for? How do you know when you win? Can we use this big fuzzy tennis ball instead of this little plastic one? And on and on. Frankly, even though I enjoy teaching kids to play Ping-Pong, it got to be tiring after a while. I grew weary of his constant barrage of questions. God, however, is never weary or impatient with our repeated requests: "The sacrifice of the wicked is an abomination to the Lord: but the prayer of the upright is his delight" (Proverbs 15:8). The prayers of his people are his constant delight because it is his Spirit who stirs us up to pray and who guides us, by his word, in what to say or ask. So Jesus bids us, "Ask, and it shall be given you; seek, and ye shall find; knock, and it shall be opened unto you: For every one that asketh receiveth; and he that seeketh findeth; and to him that knocketh it shall be opened" (Matthew 7:7–8).

There was a time in Jacob's life when he was at

the end of his rope. The time he feared had come. He must confront his brother Esau, whom he had wronged. He was terrified at the thought of being killed and began to plead with God for deliverance. Then, to prepare for the dreaded meeting, he sent his wives, servants, and sons on ahead so that he might be alone with God one last time to unburden his fearful heart.

The record then says, "And Jacob was left alone; and there wrestled a man with him until the breaking of the day" (Genesis 32:24). The secret of Jacob's success in this struggle is tucked away in one of the minor prophets. Note Hosea 12:4— "Yea, he had power over the angel, and prevailed: he wept, and made supplication unto him." Here is a strange mixture of two elements—strength and weakness. Imagine what the world would say of an Olympic athlete who wrestled like a gold medal winner yet wept like a child. Strange indeed! But that was the secret of Jacob's success. Prayers mingled with tears are the weapons with which the people of God have won powerful victories down through the centuries.

The prophet Hosea applies this truth: "Therefore turn thou to thy God: keep mercy and judgment and wait on thy God continually" (Hosea 12:6). Unlike Ephraim, who fortified himself with the worthless notion that he could rely on the help of man (Hosea 12:1), Hosea tells us to turn to God in repentance and faith—to trust him alone, to obey him and love him. Again we see the reality of a simple truth: It is the fervent, heartfelt prayer that proves to be effectual. We might ask, "How effectual? What has been accomplished through prayer?" Look at the record. Through prayer: the hail was stopped in Egypt (Exodus 9:28-33); the battle was won over Amalek (Exodus 17:11); the people were spared from the fierce wrath of God in the affair of the golden calf (Exodus 32:10-14); they were saved from the results of their murmuring and complaining (Numbers 11:1-3) and from the fiery serpents (Numbers 21:7-9); and the sun stood still (Joshua 10:12-14). We should take great encouragement from these passages as we recall that "whatsoever things were written aforetime were written for our learning, that we through patience and comfort of the scriptures might have hope" (Romans 15:4).

As we reflect upon these miracles that God has wrought in answer to prayer, and as we learn from Scripture that prayer has power to bring comfort and blessing to our lives, we could be tempted to overlook another vital aspect of prayer—the confession of our own sin to the Lord. The prayer of Daniel guides us here:

> And I set my face unto the Lord God, to seek by prayer and supplications, with fasting, and

sackcloth, and ashes: And I prayed unto the
Lord my God, and made my confession, and
said, O Lord, the great and dreadful God, keeping the covenant and mercy to them that love
him, and to them that keep his commandments;
We have sinned, and have committed iniquity,
and have done wickedly,and have rebelled, even
by departing from thy precepts and from thy
judgments. (Daniel 9:3-5)

This great prayer had its origins in the book of
Jeremiah. Daniel was studying the Scriptures when
the realization of the truth of the prophecy of
Jeremiah and its imminent fulfillment gripped his
heart (Daniel 9:1-2). That conviction led to this
great prayer of repentance and confession of sin.

Here is a great truth: God's word will help
keep us on track as we study it, apply it, and obey
it. The fact that Daniel based his prayer on the
Scriptures and received his guidance from them
should encourage us to value the word of God
above all else. I have met people in recent years
who neglected their Bibles in favor of dreams, visions, and so-called special revelations from God.
But not Daniel. Among the Old Testament prophets, Daniel was preeminent in visions and dreams;
yet he had more confidence in God's word than in
those revelations. He sat with God's word open
before him and pored over its message. And as a re-

sult, he was led to pour out his heart to the Lord in a great prayer of repentance. For guidance in confession of sin or for any other need in your life, go to the Bible.

Suppose you and two of your friends are up on a high mountain, alone. Suddenly there comes a voice from heaven that says, "Jesus Christ is the Son of God." You look at each other in amazement and inquire, "Did you hear that? Where did it come from? Up there!" You realize it is the voice of God himself. Would you be more inclined to believe the voice from heaven than you would a similar statement recorded in your Bible? If you chose the voice from heaven, Peter would tell you, "You made the wrong choice. I heard the voice of God. But my advice is to stick with your Bible." Look at his words in 2 Peter 1:16–21:

> For we have not followed cunningly devised fables, when we made known unto you the power and coming of our Lord Jesus Christ, but were eyewitnesses of his majesty. For he received from God the Father honour and glory, when there came such a voice to him from the excellent glory, This is my beloved Son, in whom I am well pleased. And this voice which came from heaven we heard, when we were with him in the holy mount. We have also a *more sure word of prophecy*; whereunto ye do well that ye take

heed, as unto a light that shineth in a dark place, until the day dawn, and the day star arise in your hearts: Knowing this first, that no prophecy of the scripture is of any private interpretation. For the prophecy came not in old time by the will of man: but holy men of God spake as they were moved by the Holy Ghost.

As I was studying that passage I asked myself, "More sure than what?" More sure than a voice from heaven? Yes, more sure than that! This is a sweeping testimony to the reliability and completeness of the word of God. So whether it be for help, encouragement, or guidance in confession and repentance, stay with the Bible. The examples of Daniel and Peter both teach us the superiority of Scripture over any other "revelation."

The Bible tells us that when Aaron entered into the holy place, he carried with him the names of the children of Israel:

And thou shalt put the two stones upon the shoulder of the ephod for stones of memorial unto the children of Israel: and Aaron shall bear their names before the Lord upon his two shoulders for a memorial. . . . And Aaron shall bear the names of the children of Israel in the breastplate of judgment upon his heart, when he goeth in unto the holy place, for a memorial before the Lord continually. (Exodus 28:12, 29)

Note where he carried them—on his shoulders and upon his heart. The names were engraved in stone. He felt the burden of his intercession for the people—just as Abraham felt the burden for the city of Sodom and for his nephew Lot, as Samuel felt the burden of prayer for the people of Israel, as Daniel felt the burden for his own sin and the sin of the people, and as Virginia and I felt the burden for Becky.

A burdened heart is one of the keys to power with God in prayer.

8
Praise and Gratitude

IN EVERY THING GIVE THANKS:
FOR THIS IS THE WILL OF GOD
IN CHRIST JESUS CONCERNING YOU.

1 Thessalonians 5:18

WHEN TRAGEDY STRIKES a well-known person and his family, it is news. Such was the case with Job. He was one of the wealthiest men in the world. He was also a truly good man. His religious life was real. Some men in his financial bracket might have used religion as a cloak to hide their shady deals, but not Job. He was a sincere follower of God. He had a fine family. The children behaved themselves. They enjoyed being with each other

101

more than running around to night spots. In short, Job was a happy man with a good life who was free from financial worries, and who loved his family, and was proud of them. And people liked him. But overnight his financial empire collapsed, and disaster struck his family. Every one of his children and all but a few of his servants died. It happened without warning. Job had no time to prepare himself emotionally for the tragedy. But his reaction was as unbelievable as the tragedy itself.

Here is the account in Scripture:

> And there was a day when his sons and his daughters were eating and drinking wine in their eldest brother's house: And there came a messenger unto Job, and said, The oxen were plowing, and the asses feeding beside them: And the Sabeans fell upon them, and took them away; yea, they have slain the servants with the edge of the sword; and I only am escaped alone to tell thee. While he was yet speaking, there came also another, and said, The fire of God is fallen from heaven, and hath burned up the sheep, and the servants, and consumed them; and I only am escaped alone to tell thee. While he was yet speaking, there came also another, and said, The Chaldeans made out three bands, and fell upon the camels, and have carried them away, yea, and slain the servants with the edge of the

> sword; and I only am escaped alone to tell thee.
> While he was yet speaking, there came also
> another, and said, Thy sons and thy daughters
> were eating and drinking wine in their eldest
> brother's house: And, behold, there came a great
> wind from the wilderness, and smote the four
> corners of the house, and it fell upon the young
> men, and they are dead; and I only am escaped
> alone to tell thee. (Job 1:13–19)

Job experienced not only financial collapse but family tragedy, and all without warning. Even Job's loving children, his primary source of human comfort, were taken from him at a time when he needed them most.

Let's try to put ourselves in Job's shoes. What would you have done if this had happened to you? Would you have lost your faith? Cursed God? Complained to God with the common cry, "Why has this happened to me?" Take a look at Job's reaction:

> Then Job arose, and rent his mantle, and shaved
> his head, and fell down upon the ground, and
> worshipped, And said, Naked came I out of my
> mother's womb, and naked shall I return thither:
> the Lord gave, and the Lord hath taken away;
> blessed be the name of the Lord. In all this Job
> sinned not, nor charged God foolishly. (Job
> 1:20–22)

He did not curse God or complain to him, but he actually worshipped and blessed the name of the Lord. Here was the richest man in the country reduced to poverty, bowing down before the Lord in a spirit of praise and submission. No doubt Job had been in the habit of thanking God for all his goodness, and this sudden radical turn of events did not change his thankful nature. Thanksgiving was Job's lifestyle, part of his character. Now, in this time of suffering and tragedy, he did not turn away from God, because praise and thanksgiving were ingrained in his life.

Paul's admonition to the Thessalonians speaks to this point: "Rejoice evermore. Pray without ceasing. In everything give thanks: for this is the will of God in Christ Jesus concerning you" (1 Thessalonians 5:16–18). Our joy and thanksgiving cannot be shaken if they are rooted in the character of God and our rich fellowship with him. Philippians 4:4 is not an impossible ideal. When Paul says, "Rejoice in the Lord always: and again I say, Rejoice," he knows this commandment is well within the possibility of the Christian's experience if he has learned to give thanks in everything (1 Thessalonians 5:18). God enables us to live a life of constant joy, unceasing prayer, and heartfelt thanks through Jesus Christ. In fact, he uses bitter circumstances, trials, and afflictions to deepen our love for him and strengthen our faith in him.

Virginia and I have watched this process at work in our lives. For some years we have lived with a deep heartache, which seems to have no termination date. It would be easier to face a difficulty if we knew it would end by next Wednesday or next month or next year. We could brace up, tighten our belts, and endure. It is more difficult to thank God in the midst of suffering when there is no end in sight. But it is not impossible. It has become clear to us over the years that God has used this experience to deepen our devotion, strengthen our faith, and purify our lives. For that trial and many other things, we can give him thanks. God has used these trials to balance out our prayer life. Prayer time that used to be taken up solely with petitions for ourselves is now meshed with thanksgiving.

I was staggered by a question that the Lord brought to my mind recently while reading Luke 17. When the question first came to mind, I dismissed it as impossible. But the more I pondered the question, the more disturbed I became. It comes from the incident of the ten lepers in Luke 17:11-19:

> And it came to pass, as he went to Jerusalem, that he passed through the midst of Samaria and Galilee. And as he entered into a certain village, there met him ten men that were lepers, which stood afar off: And they lifted up their voices, and said, Jesus, Master, have mercy on us. And

when he saw them, he said unto them, Go shew yourselves unto the priests. And it came to pass, that, as they went, they were cleansed. And one of them, when he saw that he was healed, turned back, and with a loud voice glorified God, and fell down on his face at his feet, giving him thanks: and he was a Samaritan. And Jesus answering said, Were there not ten cleansed? but where arc the nine? There are not found that returned to give glory to God, save this stranger. And he said unto him, Arise, go thy way: thy faith hath made thee whole.

Here is the question that staggered me: Does this passage teach that gratitude is more rare than faith? Ten lepers were cleansed, and only one returned to thank Jesus. All ten of them had the faith to act in obedience to the word of Christ, but only one returned to give thanks. Faith is rare. Jesus asked, in fact, "When the son of man returns, will he find faith on the earth?" But it seems that gratitude is even rarer than faith. How many truly thankful people do you know? I don't know very many.

But the word of God commands: "In *every thing* give thanks: for this is the will of God in Christ Jesus concerning you" (1 Thessalonians 5:18). *Everything?* Yes, everything. Give thanks for the good times. Give thanks for the hard times.

If we did that, every aspect of our lives would be transformed. We would think differently, talk differently, and act differently. A truly thankful spirit would radically change our lifestyle. It would also change our prayer life. We would experience Philippians 4:6-7—"Be careful for nothing; but in every thing by prayer and supplication with thanksgiving let your requests be made known unto God. And the peace of God, which passeth all understanding, shall keep your hearts and minds through Christ Jesus." Thanksgiving for past blessings is the dynamic base upon which to build a strong prayer life, and upon which to make requests for the future.

The Psalms have been called "The Prayer Book of the Bible." It is certainly no accident that the Psalms are divided almost equally between petitions, and thanksgiving and praise. The Psalms give the clearest guidance for a lifestyle of thanksgiving: "It is a good thing to give thanks unto the Lord, and to sing praises unto thy name, O most High: To shew forth thy lovingkindness in the morning, and thy faithfulness every night" (Psalm 92:1-2).

Suppose you had no money, no food, and no place to live. Suppose a wealthy man searched you out and offered you the use of his palatial mansion. You could live there rent free. The refrigerator and freezer contained enough food to last for months.

All he requested from you was a thank-you note each month. Do you think you would take him up on his offer? Of course you would.

God has done exactly that for us. He has given us his beautiful world to live in. He has promised to meet our needs. Our response? "O give thanks unto the Lord; call upon his name; make known his deeds among the people" (Psalm 105:1). To thank the Lord is our small response to the great things he has done for us.

Look at your prayers. Do they reflect a thankful spirit? We are called often to thank the Lord. "O give thanks unto the Lord, for he is good: for his mercy endureth for ever. O give thanks unto the God of gods: for his mercy endureth for ever. O give thanks to the Lord of lords: for his mercy endureth for ever" (Psalm 136:1–3).

The Psalms tell us how to develop a thanksgiving lifestyle. But the greatest challenge is the lifestyle of Jesus himself. When Jesus fed the five thousand, what did he do? He took the seven loaves and *gave thanks*. What did he do at the resurrection of Lazarus from the dead? "Then they took away the stone from the place where the dead was laid. And Jesus lifted up his eyes, and said, Father, *I thank thee* that thou hast heard me" (John 11:41). And at the last supper "He took the cup, and *gave thanks*" (Matthew 26:27).

If we want to be true disciples, we must do

what Hebrews 13:15 tells us to do: "By him therefore let us offer the *sacrifice of praise* to God continually, that is, the fruit of our lips *giving thanks* to his name." Your prayer life, if it is to grow in effectiveness and power, must be filled with the sound of a thankful heart.

9
Oneness of Heart

AGAIN I SAY UNTO YOU, THAT
IF TWO OF YOU SHALL AGREE ON EARTH
AS TOUCHING ANY THING THAT THEY SHALL
ASK, IT SHALL BE DONE FOR THEM
OF MY FATHER WHICH IS IN HEAVEN.

Matthew 18:19

IN LATE SPRING of 1978 my wife and I met our son Randy in Bombay, India. We had been in Asia for a few months and were on our way to the Middle East, Eastern Europe, and eventually Western Europe. After a week or so in India, the three of us left for Iran. Upon our arrival in Teheran it became evident that Randy had picked up a virus in India. He began to lose weight. We administered the medicines we carried, but they didn't help.

After a week or so in Iran, we went to Istanbul. There we consulted a Turkish doctor who examined Randy and informed us he had cholera. He gave Randy five different medicines, and he assured us they would kill whatever was causing the problem.

We went from Istanbul to Sofia, Bulgaria, where we remained about a week, and then flew to Bucharest, Romania. By this time three weeks had passed. Randy had lost about fifteen pounds, and he had become extremely ill. We were deeply concerned. We prayed much, but no relief came. What to do? Should we cancel the rest of the ministry tour? Should we send Randy off to friends in England or Germany to see what they could do?

I visited the Pan American airlines office and discovered there was a plane leaving in two days for Frankfurt, Germany. Should we take it? We still had about three weeks left in our schedule to visit Yugoslavia, Poland, and Czechoslavakia. After some more time in prayer I told Virginia and Randy how I thought the Lord was leading us. If Randy were not better in two days, we would take the Pan Am flight to Frankfurt. The medicines the Turkish doctor had given us obviously were doing no good, so I decided to seek further medical help in Bucharest. I was informed there was a clinic which would see us and was given directions to get there.

As we approached the clinic we had to walk

past the American Embassy, and I suggested we go into the Embassy and get some information about the clinic. The young Marine at the front desk warned me against the clinic. "Don't go in there!" he said, "They will kill you. They are twenty years behind the West in medical technology. Wait a minute. I'll call an Embassy nurse and see if she will talk to you." She wasn't in, so he said to come back in an hour.

When we returned, we were ushered immediately into the nurse's office. Her first words were, "How did you get in to see me? I don't see tourists. My job is with the Embassy personnel." I told her about my conversation with the Marine, explained the nature of our work, and stressed that we weren't exactly tourists. "Okay," she said, "Tell me the problem." We told her all about it and showed her the medicines the Turkish doctor had given us. She discovered that some were out of date, and one was not even listed in her medical book. Her first act was to throw them all away. Then she gave Randy a shot to prevent hepatitis and a bottle of Kaopectate and told us to call the next day if the problem had not cleared up.

We went back to the hotel and had lunch. No problem. Lunch again. No problem. We had breakfast. No problem. Lunch again. No problem. Randy was cured. We went to prayer and thanked the Lord. God had heard us when we had agreed in prayer and had guided us in a marvelous and exciting way to the help we needed. People with united hearts, on their knees together before the throne of grace, experience a power with God that results in remarkable answers to prayer.

A beautiful picture of this oneness of heart in prayer is painted for us in Acts 1:13–14.

> And when they were come in, they went up into an upper room, where abode both Peter, and James, and John, and Andrew, Philip, and Thomas, Bartholomew, and Matthew, James the son of Alphaeus, and Simon Zelotes, and Judas the brother of James. These all continued with one accord in prayer and supplication, with the women, and Mary the mother of Jesus, and with his brethren.

The activities in that room produced no discordant vibrations. There was a God-given love between them and a God-given objective in their prayers.

This unity had not always prevailed among the disciples. Formerly there had been strife and occasional power struggles. Those were the learning years in the school of Christ, as he taught them to walk in the Spirit. But now we hear no more of that. They are on their knees together: "And when they heard that, they lifted up their voice to God with one accord, and said, Lord, thou art God, which hast made heaven, and earth, and the sea, and all that in them is" (Acts 4:24). "One accord" does not mean that they were mouthing the same words, but that they were together in heart. This is a lovely scene. Most of these people had known each other for years. They had listened to Jesus, followed him, and lived through the events of his death, burial, and resurrection. They had watched him die. They saw him alive after the resurrection. These experiences had welded their hearts together as one.

Although many thousands of new believers soon joined their ranks, the Christians maintained their early unity during this period of rapid growth: "And the multitude of them that believed were of one heart and of one soul: neither said any of them that ought of the things which he possessed was his own; but they had all things common" (Acts 4:32). Love and sacrificial giving prevailed. The fellowship of believers was open to all races and social classes.

There are churches and pastors today who fear growth, especially if it means bringing in people who are racially, socially, or economically "different." They have a cozy fellowship; members get along well; there is love and brotherhood. And they fear that if they go out and bring in sinners off the streets their pleasant little group will be shattered. The early church faced this same problem, but their unity and the power of the Holy Spirit melted it. If our ancestors in the faith overcame this problem, so can we. Pray over Acts 4:32, and ask God to fulfill it in your assembly.

I am impressed by how often in the Bible the importance of unity among believers is stressed. Jesus prayed for it:

> That they all may be one; as thou, Father, art in me, and I in thee, that they also may be one in us: that the world may believe that thou hast sent me. And the glory which thou gavest me I have given them; that they may be one, even as we are one: I in them, and thou in me, that they may be made perfect in one; and that the world may know that thou hast sent me, and hast loved them, as thou hast loved me. (John 17:21–23)

Jesus is not speaking about an *organizational* unity, but an *organic* one. The common element is the love of God and the fellowship in the Scriptures, not a constitution or a set of rules. We love, because the Father first loved us, with the same love that he has for his only begotten Son! We have become partakers of the divine nature; therefore, we can be one, just as the Father and the Son are one. But this unity is only possible in Christ. Our union with him can result in a union with one another that is so real and so remarkable that even the pagan world around us will acknowledge that it is supernatural. Christ's prayer corresponds to the new commandment he had given: "A new commandment I give unto you, that ye love one another; as I have loved you, that ye also love one another. By this shall all men know that ye are my disciples, if ye have love one to another" (John 13:34–35). Jesus called this commandment new, not because the *idea* of love was new, but because the *direction* of the love was new. It is outward looking, extended not just to those of the same nation, but to every person in every nation who belongs to the family of God.

The love he commanded did not only possess a new dimension, but also a new *intensity*. It was to be "as I have loved you." This supernatural love not only draws believers to each other but gives them a continuing powerful witness to the world. Christ's love abiding in us and flowing through us is easily recognized. It cannot be humanly produced, but must come from Christ alone. There were all sorts of laws on the Jewish books that outlined the proper course to follow in obtaining revenge and retaliating for a wrong. The world was filled with self-love and the means to promote it. But Jesus had walked among them as one who served. He had washed their feet. He would soon die for them. *This* concept was new!

People of the world know nothing of such love but are drawn to it when they see it in action.

When this love controls the hearts of believers, it will draw them ever closer to one another. But such love can only flourish in a climate of intimate fellowship with Christ. And for that Christ prayed. One of the great vehicles to carry this message of God's gospel to the world is the beauty of transformed lives manifesting God's love. This kind of "incarnation" of God's love in the lives of his disciples requires a growing fellowship between Christ and his disciples. The eternal salvation of millions of people depends on this manifestation of love. This is one reason why Christ poured out his heart in prayer for oneness among his people.

This kind of love results in a servant's attitude. The apostle Paul details the relationship between love and humility: "Fulfil ye my joy, that ye be likeminded, having the same love, being of one accord, of one mind. Let nothing be done through strife or vainglory; but in lowliness of mind let each esteem other better than themselves" (Philippians 2:2–3). This was one of the first verses that Dawson Trotman told me to memorize when I began to associate with The Navigators in the autumn of 1949. After carrying this verse on the table of my heart for over thirty years, I am finally beginning to see some of the deeper implications of this passage. To esteem others "better" than myself does not mean they are manifestly superior to me in most things, but that I must look upon them through the eyes of a servant. They are worthy of my time, my prayers, my life. Selfish ambition and a bloated opinion of myself destroy any reflection of Christ in me and make for strife. Peace and oneness cannot coexist with selfishness and pride. I must get a clear picture of my own insignificance compared to the glory of Christ and his mission in the world, and I can only maintain such a vision if I am in regular fellowship with Christ through the Scriptures and prayer.

In the winter of 1981 America witnessed the heartbreak of a tragic plane crash in the Potomac River in Washington, D.C. As news began to filter out, we became aware of a person the rescue teams began to call "the sixth man." Five people were pulled to safety as rescue ropes and life preservers were dropped to them from helicopters that hovered overhead. The rescuers watched in wonder as one of those in the water repeatedly handed off the ring to others around him. Finally, when five were lifted to safety the helicopter returned for the sixth man, but he was gone. He had slipped beneath the icy waters and drowned. He had literally esteemed others better than himself.

This dramatic demonstration of heroism and sacrifice is an illustration of what Paul was pleading for in the daily life of the believer. Living for others is the pathway to peace, brotherhood, and true oneness in love. Jesus said, "Greater love hath no man than this, that a man lay down his life for his friends" (John 15:13).

Oneness of spirit and unity of heart among believers will smother the evil weeds of competition. In his letters, Paul sounds this theme repeatedly. He urges the Romans, "Let us therefore follow after the things which make for peace, and things wherewith one may edify another" (Romans 14:19). We cannot build each other up if we are bickering among ourselves. We must concentrate on the things that promote peace—humility, sacrifice, a servant spirit, self-denial, and love.

Don't argue over things that are insignificant. Overlook the foolish acts of those young in the faith, and help them grow to maturity. Strive together with a holy zeal in those things that truly matter. The phrase *follow after* means "to pursue diligently," much as a scientist would who is on the brink of a discovery that will cure a foul disease and bring healing and relief to millions. Paul uses the same word when he says, "I *press* toward the mark" (Philippians 3:14). Peter uses this word: "Let him seek peace and *pursue* it" (1 Peter 3:11, *The New Scofield Reference Bible*). Oneness of heart can be elusive, but we must capture and retain it if we are to fulfill our highest calling in life—the glory of God: "Now the God of patience and consolation grant you to be like-minded one toward another according to Christ Jesus: that ye may with one mind and one mouth glorify God, even the Father of our Lord Jesus Christ" (Romans 15:5-6).

In Paul's first letter to the Corinthians unity was the first topic on the agenda when he really got down to the crux of their problem. "Now I beseech you, brethren, by the name of our Lord Jesus Christ, that ye all speak the same thing, and that there be no divisions among you; but that ye be perfectly joined together in the same mind and in the same judgment" (1 Corinthians 1:10). His appeal to them is based not on their love for himself, not on what their pagan neighbors would think, but on their regard for the name of our Lord Jesus Christ. And his call to them is not just to improve a little in this matter, but to be a model of excellence, to be "perfectly joined together." He uses a word here that pictures a person fine-tuning a piano. He wants no discordant notes. His goal for them is a rhapsody that will thrill the soul of the world. This is the first major theme in his message to this church, and it is also the last. At the end of his second letter he says: "Finally, brethren, farewell. Be perfect, be of good comfort, *be of one mind*, live in peace; and the God of love and peace shall be with you" (2 Corinthians 13:11).

Paul understood the implications of fights among the believers. The gospel message could be nullified by fleshly activities. Occasionally, in his letters to the church, he singles out individual members of the congregation for a personal exhortation to unity. Two women were the recipients of such a reminder: "I beseech Euodias, and beseech Syntyche, that they be of the same mind in the Lord" (Philippians 4:2). We are not told what the specific problem was. Possibly they were vying with each other for social preeminence. Maybe they were both after the same man. Possibly they were trying to thwart the plans of the congregation. Whatever it was, Paul wanted it to stop.

Peter also stresses the importance of unity: "Finally, *be ye all of one mind*, having compassion one of another, love as brethren, be pitiful, be courteous" (1 Peter 3:8). Peter's words remind us of the statement of James:

> But if ye have bitter envying and strife in your hearts, glory not, and lie not against the truth. This wisdom descendeth not from above, but is earthly, sensual, devilish. For where envying and strife is, there is confusion and every evil work. But the wisdom that is from above is first pure, then peaceable, gentle, and easy to be intreated, full of mercy and good fruits, without partiality, and without hypocrisy. And the fruit of righteousness is sown in peace of them that make peace. (James 3:14–18)

One aspect of unity is that it brings strength to our lives. Ecclesiastes 4:9–12 says,

> Two are better than one; because they have a
> good reward for their labour. For if they fall, the
> one will lift up his fellow: but woe to him that is
> alone when he falleth; for he hath not another to
> help him up. Again, if two lie together, then they
> have heat: but how can one be warm alone? And
> if one prevail against him, two shall withstand
> him; and a threefold cord is not quickly broken.

Two things stand out in the passage: Unity brings mutual strength and safety, and a close companion can help keep me from falling. Alone, I am exposed to temptations that do not affect me when I am with a companion. In our Navigator summer conference program we encourage conferees to go hiking in pairs. If one were to fall and twist an ankle or break a leg, there would be someone there to help.

When I graduated from Marine Boot Camp in 1943, our drill instructor encouraged us to go on liberty in pairs. If some sailor or soldier got drunk and wanted to pick a fight with us Marines we could help each other out. Similarly, many swimming instructors encourage the buddy system. As one keeps an eye on the other, there is less of a chance for an accident to occur. One of the finest examples in Scripture of the buddy system is 1 Samuel 23:16—"And Jonathan Saul's son arose, and went to David into the wood, and strengthened his hand in God." While David was hiding from Saul, Jonathan, David's closest friend, came to encourage him. He directed David's thoughts to the Lord as his source of strength, confidence, and counsel. Although David was a mighty man of God, even he needed help from a friend. No doubt Jonathan reminded David of the promises God had made to him and the many times in David's life when God had proved his faithfulness.

David gives us another powerful reason for living in oneness of heart with our brothers and sisters in Christ—it brings us pleasure:

> Behold, how good and how pleasant it is for brethren to dwell together in unity! It is like the precious ointment upon the head, that ran down upon the beard, even Aaron's beard: that went down to the skirts of his garments, As the dew of Hermon, and as the dew that descended upon the mountains of Zion: for there the Lord commanded the blessing, even life for evermore. (Psalm 133)

This unity of spirit is likened to the fragrant oil that covered the head of Aaron the priest. David says when unity of heart is present there is also the evident blessing of God.

I have observed this blessed unity happening in Christian service. When God's people are striving together with one heart and soul, their efforts are accompanied by the Lord's blessing on their work, *and they are happy*. Unity is one of the keys that unlocks the power of God in our midst. When we serve together in love, the God of love and peace showers his blessing on us in a "pleasant" way.

I have found five passages in the Bible that give clear instruction on how we can enjoy unbroken unity of heart. Let's begin with Isaiah 52:8—"Thy watchmen shall lift up the voice; with the voice together shall they sing: for they shall see eye to eye, when the Lord shall bring again Zion." When you and I see "eye to eye," or agree with God regarding his objectives for the world and his desires for his people, we see eye to eye with each other as well. The key to being in tune with our brothers is for all of us to be in tune with God. All of our plans, programs, activities, and worship must be centered in God. When that is the case, God's people enjoy true unity.

The second key to unity is found in Philippians 3:16—"Nevertheless, whereto we have already attained, *let us walk by the same rule*, let us mind the same thing." Not only must we be striving toward the same end; but we must also be playing by the same rules. Try to visualize the confusion that would prevail on an athletic field if each player on a team played by a different set of rules—one by the rules of rugby, another by the rules of American football, another by the rules of soccer, and still another by the rules of tennis. The result would be total disarray. Our only rule of faith and life is the Bible. When we search the Scriptures together and get our plans and programs from God's word, we will experience the kind of unity that pleases God.

First Corinthians 12:12 talks about unity in diversity: "For as the body is one, and hath many members, and all the members of that one body, being many, are one body: so also is Christ." It helps to remember that we are a body made up of different parts with a diversity of functions. The ear does not look like the foot nor have the same function, but each needs the other. Christ and his church make up one body with many members. If I am the little toe on the left foot, I have no right to expect all other members of that body to look like me or to function like me. But our differences do not destroy our unity; they *establish* it—we all need each other. It is when I begin to insist that each member do what I do that discord arises.

Nature teaches us that different functions are necessary within a single organism. A rose bush would look strange indeed if it were one big root or one gigantic petal or one large leaf. In the church also there are different callings and gifts. Unity comes when we remember we are a body with members who look different and function differently. We can then thank the Lord for our fellow Christian rather than complain about him.

Another key ingredient in unity is a forgiving spirit: "Let all bitterness, and wrath, and anger, and clamour, and evil speaking, be put away from you, with all malice: And be ye kind one to another, tenderhearted, forgiving one another, even as God for Christ's sake hath forgiven you" (Ephesians 4:31–32). Forgiveness is Christlike. Remember Christ's words in Luke 23:34—"Father, forgive them." To forgive is to wash the chalkboard clean, to pardon the offender and forget the offense. But it is hard to forgive others, because there is something gratifying to the flesh to remember, to know you were right, to feel hurt and wounded, to walk around with a very legitimate chip on your shoulder—as the French say, "to have a tooth against someone"—to know full well that he shouldn't have said those words or treated us that way, to insist that he had no right to do what he did. Even though these things may be true, the Bible says that I do not have the right to fight back or harbor a grudge. Remember and obey Ephesians 4:32. My responsibility is to forgive and forget. Hard to do, you say? Of course! But ask God to help you. Forgiveness lies directly in the path of peace and unity.

The fifth key to unity is found in Philippians 1:27—"Only let your conversation be as it becometh the gospel of Christ: that whether I come and see you, or else be absent, I may hear of your affairs, that ye stand fast in one spirit, with one mind striving together for the faith of the gospel." When I am striving together with my brother in some grand and meaningful enterprise, I am not striving against him. The greatest enterprise I know is carrying out the Great Commission of Jesus Christ. When I am shoulder to shoulder with my brother, striving together for the faith of the gospel, I am not even thinking of picking a fight with him. We have a common enemy—Satan.

Israel is constantly characterized in the Old Testament as a murmuring, bickering, stiff-necked people. Why? I believe it was because they had forgotten their God-given mission. God had said:

> Now therefore, if ye will obey my voice indeed, and keep my covenant, then ye shall be a peculiar treasure unto me above all people: for all the earth is mine: And ye shall be unto me a kingdom of priests, and an holy nation. These are the words which thou shalt speak unto the children of Israel. (Exodus 19:5-6)

The whole earth and all its people belong to God. He had picked Israel for a spiritual ministry to all the nations, and had taken them to his heart in order that through them he might bless the world. But they failed to see themselves in this light—as a servant nation to the world. They tried, rather, to monopolize for themselves that which really belonged to the rest of humanity. They became ingrown and self-centered. Their hardness of heart sparked one of the great tragedies of history—the failure of the Jews to spread the kingdom of God to the Gentile nations.

Any church group can become self-serving. It can get wrapped up in its own activities and forget its primary mission—the evangelization of the world. In the book of Acts evangelizing was not one of a number of important things; it was *the* important thing. Everything else was subordinate to this main thrust. If a group or a church loses sight of this objective and becomes ingrown, its members get caught up in secondary matters and soon find things to quarrel about. It is easy to strive with each other in such an atmosphere. When a group like this tries to pray, nothing much happens because they can't agree on anything important.

Stagnation can happen to a congregation, to a denomination, to a parachurch group, to a family. Recently I was in the home of a couple who have been married for about fifteen years. I saw on a shelf a number of old books—books on devotion to God, witnessing, prayer, and so on. Then I looked over the new books that were there. They were on such themes as how to be happy, how to be secure, how to have a successful marriage, how to have happy children. I asked myself, "Have they become ingrown?" I am not opposed to happy homes and happy families; I want that for myself. I would rather have a happy wife than a morose one. But as I looked over that stack of books, it occurred to me there was nothing on the *mission* of the family to be a light in the neighborhood and in the world. Nothing draws a family closer than to realize that they have been placed in a neighborhood to share the gospel—to plan together and pray together to tell the good news to their friends and neighbors. That's what Paul was getting at when he spoke of standing fast "in one spirit, with one mind striving together for the faith of the gospel."

These five key passages have helped me learn how to develop the unity that pleases God. It has not been easy or automatic. I find that it's one of those things that requires constant attention. Paul called it an "endeavor."

> I therefore, the prisoner of the Lord, beseech you that ye walk worthy of the vocation wherewith ye are called. With all lowliness and meekness, with longsuffering, forbearing one another in love; *endeavouring* to keep the unity of the Spirit in the bond of peace. (Ephesians 4:1–3)

He also referred to it as a fight:

> For I would that ye knew what great *conflict* I have for you, and for them at Laodicea, and for

as many as have not seen my face in the flesh;
That their hearts might be comforted, *being knit
together in love*, and unto all riches of the full
assurance of understanding, to the acknowledgment of the mystery of God, and of the Father,
and of Christ. (Colossians 2:1–2)

Paul's concern and care for these people actually amounted to a conflict. He agonized over
them even as he "travailed" for the Galatians. And
what was the objective of Paul's spiritual warfare
on behalf of the believers? Was it their happiness or
financial security? No, it was that they might be
"knit together in love."

Jesus linked unity of heart with worship.

Ye have heard that it was said by them of old
time, Thou shalt not kill; and whosoever shall
kill shall be in danger of judgment: But I say
unto you, That whosoever is angry with his
brother without a cause shall be in danger of the
judgment: and whosoever shall say to his
brother, Raca, shall be in danger of the council:
but whosoever shall say, Thou fool, shall be in
danger of hell fire. Therefore if thou bring thy
gift to the altar, and there rememberest that thy
brother hath ought against thee; Leave there thy
gift before the altar, and go thy way; first be
reconciled to thy brother, and then come and offer thy gift. (Matthew 5:21–24)

Jesus pictures a man who has arrived at the altar with his gift, and while he is there, about to offer his gift to God, he is reminded that he has offended his brother and that this wrong has never been set right. Jesus tells him to leave the gift at the altar— leave the place of worship—go find his brother, and get things straightened out. This principle is true whether we have been the offender or the victim: "Moreover if thy brother shall trespass against thee, go and tell him his fault between thee and him alone: if he shall hear thee, thou hast gained thy brother" (Matthew 18:15).

Rather than harbor resentment in our hearts over an offense, we should go to our brother (or sister) and clear it up. There must be nothing left unforgiven that the devil can use to destroy the unity of the brotherhood. The effectiveness of our prayer life depends on it: "And when ye stand praying, forgive, if ye have ought against any: that your Father also which is in heaven may forgive you your trespasses" (Mark 11:25). A disciple cannot pray with confidence if an unforgiving spirit lurks in his heart. If such a spirit is allowed to remain, it breaks his fellowship with God and man. The qualification for prevailing prayer is that we are at peace with God and men. Jesus insisted on this. One of his great designs was to see his people living together in harmony and love. As those who know their need for daily cleansing from God, let us take to heart the words of Christ. "For if ye forgive men their trespasses, your heavenly Father will also forgive you: But if ye forgive not men their trespasses, neither will your Father forgive your trespasses" (Matthew 6:14–15). You cannot be cleansed from your daily sins while harboring an unforgiving spirit.

10
Perseverance

AND HE SPAKE A PARABLE
UNTO THEM TO THIS END, THAT MEN OUGHT
ALWAYS TO PRAY, AND NOT TO FAINT.

Luke 18:1

MY FIRST ANSWER to prayer was a small miracle. It was about 3:30 p.m. on Friday afternoon. I was not scheduled to get off work until 4:00 p.m., and I wanted to go home to Council Bluffs, Iowa. I was working for the railroad, and the train I wanted to take was standing at the station ready to leave in about fifteen minutes—which was fifteen minutes before I was scheduled to get off work. If I missed it, I would have to wait to catch the midnight freight train. I asked the station agent if I could leave a few minutes early, and he said, "Yes, just close up and put a seal on the LCL freight car, and you can leave." And that was my problem.

I had opened the car that morning, and it had taken a good half hour. The door was banged-up and rusty. I had used a long steel wrecking bar to pry it open inch by inch. I knew I could not get the door closed before the train left, and I was angry. Why hadn't the stupid train been a few minutes late, as it usually was? Why hadn't the boss told me earlier to close up the freight car? And for that matter, why couldn't someone else close the dumb car? But no. I had to do it, and I knew it couldn't be done in time to catch the train.

As I walked to the car, however, a novel and exciting thought entered my head. Why not pray and ask God to close the door? He was strong. He could do it easily. I had been a Christian a few days, and I hadn't asked him to do much of anything yet. Why not pray and see what he would do? So I did. "God, I'd like to get on that train, and I need your help. I've got to close that door, but I can't do it. It will take too long. So, God, would you please shut that door?" With that, I reached up with one hand, pulled on the door, and it rolled shut like it was riding on ball-bearing roller skates. I snapped the seal in place, walked over to the train, and went home.

That was over thirty years ago. I've learned a lot about prayer and have received many answers to prayer in these thirty years, but there has been none more direct and dramatic than that first one when I was a brand-new babe in Christ just a few days old in the Lord.

One of the key lessons I have learned about prayer is that God does not always answer our prayer immediately. Sometimes we pray a long time before the answer comes. There are a couple of things that I have prayed for for years, and there is still no answer. But I have not lost heart, and I am still praying. That's the theme of this chapter—perseverance in prayer.

One passage on perseverance that has blessed me is the parable of Jesus in Luke 18:1–8:

> And he spake a parable unto them to this end, that men ought always to pray, and not to faint; Saying, There was in a city a judge, which feared not God, neither regarded man: And there was a widow in that city; and she came unto him, saying, Avenge me of mine adversary. And he would not for a while: but afterward he said within himself, Though I fear not God, nor regard man; Yet because this widow troubleth me, I will avenge her, lest by her continual coming she weary me. And the Lord said, Hear what the unjust judge saith. And shall not God avenge his

own elect, which cry day and night unto him,
though he bear long with them? I tell you that he
will avenge them speedily. Nevertheless when
the Son of man cometh, shall he find faith on the
earth?

The true meaning of some of Jesus' parables is often
buried in the middle of the story, requiring some
thought and analysis to dig it out. But with this one
the meaning is right up front: "Men ought always
to pray and not to faint." And then he goes on to
show how it was the perseverance of the widow
that caused the unjust judge to act.

There are a number of insights in this parable
that encourage our prayer life. For instance, the
widow was a total stranger to the judge, whereas
we are God's children (John 1:12). The widow
came to one whom Jesus describes as an unjust
judge. But when you and I approach the throne of
grace, we come to a "righteous Father" (John
17:25), "our Father which art in Heaven" (Luke
11:2). The widow came all alone with no one to
help her plead her cause. By contrast, "We have an
advocate with the Father, Jesus Christ the righteous" (1 John 2:1). The widow was a bother and
nuisance to the judge. But we never "bother" God
with our prayers. His plea is, "Call unto me"
(Jeremiah 33:3).

There are two primary teachings in this parable of Jesus: We must persevere—continue to pray. We also must not lose heart or give up.

A number of passages in the Bible instruct us in what persevering prayer is, why we should engage in it, and how to do it. Luke 11:5–8 illustrates the value of importunity:

> And he said unto them, Which of you shall have a friend, and shall go unto him at midnight, and say unto him, Friend, lend me three loaves; For a friend of mine in his journey is come to me, and I have nothing to set before him? And he from within shall answer and say, Trouble me not: the door is now shut, and my children are with me in bed; I cannot rise and give thee. I say unto you, Though he will not rise and give him, because he is his friend, yet because of his importunity he will rise and give him as many as he needeth.

Jesus here elevates prayer to the level of personal friendship with God. What an amazing privilege! Millions of people see God as an unknowable, unpredictable, unfriendly power out there somewhere of whom they live in fear and uncertainty. In this passage the man went to his friend for help at an inconvenient and unusual hour. It must have been a serious emergency. If the man had been walking all day and hadn't arrived until midnight, he was no doubt famished. He needed something to eat. But the man with the bread also had a problem. The houses in that part of the world didn't have separate bedrooms. The parents would toss down the mats on the floor and bolt the door before the family went to sleep. To walk around the room, get the food, unbolt the door, and get the food to the man would wake the children. And you know what a circus it is when all the kids wake up in the middle of the night. But because his friend was banging on the door and shouting, it was less trouble for him to give the man the bread.

The next two verses hammer home Jesus' point:

> And I say unto you, Ask, and it shall be given you; seek, and ye shall find; knock, and it shall be opened unto you, For everyone that asketh receiveth; and he that seeketh findeth; and to him that knocketh it shall be opened. (Luke 11:9–10)

The conditions: ask, seek, and knock—three words that are the heartbeat of perseverance. And then the promise—"every one." No exceptions. No doubts. What was it that secured the answer? Perseverance.

Another passage that sheds light on this matter is Luke 21:34–36:

> And take heed to yourselves, lest at any time

> your hearts be overcharged with surfeiting, and
> drunkenness, and the cares of this life, and so
> that day come upon you unawares. For as a
> snare shall it come on all them that dwell on the
> face of the whole earth. Watch ye therefore, and
> pray always, that ye may be accounted worthy
> to escape all these things that shall come to pass,
> and to stand before the Son of man.

The appetites of the flesh and the cares of this world are powerful forces that we must deal with constantly. Our own inner corruption can betray us and lure us down the wrong path. The cares of this life can crush us and immobilize us in our walk of faith. How can we withstand this two-fold pressure? Jesus says that constant watchful prayer will enable us to resist fainting: "Men ought *always* to pray, and not to faint." He is talking about consistent persevering prayer. Jesus is referring here to a very specific and difficult time in history, but we can apply the passage to difficult times in general. We prepare for the tough times in our lives by cultivating a daily time of communion with the Lord. A prayerless life cannot cope with the attacks of corruption within and crushing blows from without.

Some friends of ours recently faced some devastating blows from the enemy. Their car was stolen; their daughter was attacked by deep doubts and fears; the wife had some physical difficulties that almost took her life; they were facing the possibility of a move that, because of schooling and job opportunities, would have split the family right down the middle. As I watched them face these trials, one word came to my mind again and again: "Victory!" Here was a family facing some very unusual difficulties. And here was a family living in victory. A look behind the scene revealed the reason: consistent, persevering, importunate prayer.

David gives a clear, concise message to all who face the battles of life: "As for me, I will call upon God; and the Lord shall save me. Evening, and morning, and at noon, will I pray, and cry aloud: and he shall hear my voice" (Psalm 55:16–17). Note that he does not try to match wits with his enemies or meet force with force. His first reaction is to call upon God. His testimony is a word of faith: "The Lord shall save me." But he is careful to explain that his concept of prayer is not that of a hasty, brief prayer at a convenient time. He speaks of evening, morning, and noon. His meaning is clear. Begin the day with God; live the day with God; end the day with God. David is absolutely confident of the outcome. God will hear. God will answer. Persevering prayer will prevail.

Thank God for the renewed interest in prayer in many churches throughout the world. Prayer meetings are alive and vital. Prayer conferences are being held. In our own ministry The Navigators have made prayer our number one imperative for the 1980s.

There is a discouraging element, however, in some current teaching on prayer. The impression is sometimes given that God hears and answers the prayers of his people because of their spiritual strength and impeccable walk in the Spirit. But note that the basis of David's heartfelt and persevering prayer was his weakness:

> Bow down thine ear, O Lord, hear me: for *I am poor and needy*. Preserve my soul; for I am holy: O thou my God, save thy servant that trusteth in thee. Be merciful unto me, O Lord: for I cry unto thee daily. Rejoice the soul of thy servant: for unto thee, O Lord, do I lift up my soul. For thou, Lord, art good, and *ready to forgive*; and plenteous in mercy unto all them that call upon thee. Give ear, O Lord, unto my prayer; and attend to the voice of my supplications. In *the day of my trouble* I will call upon thee: for thou wilt answer me. (Psalm 86:1–7)

He asks for God's ear *because he is poor and needy*. He sees himself as a helpless sinner in need of God's mercy and forgiveness. Therefore he will call, and God will hear and answer. A believer's cry for help will never go unheeded.

The unique compassion and greatness of God shines through the lines of Psalm 102:16–17: "When the Lord shall build up Zion, he shall appear in his glory. He will regard the prayer of the destitute, and not despise their prayer." Try to imagine the picture created by these words. A mighty ruler appears in splendor, busily involved in rebuilding his capital city. He must take care of hundreds of details and make momentous decisions. He probably would have no time to hear and act upon the plea of a destitute individual in the crowd. But the Lord does. He is robed in the splendor of light and purity. He is busily engaged day and night in building his Kingdom. But he always listens to the cry of the poorest and neediest of his people.

Psalm 142:4–5 tenderly whispers the powerful truth that God cares for us and answers our cries —when all human help fails: "I looked on my right hand, and beheld, but there was no man that would know me: refuge failed me; no man cared for my soul. I cried unto thee, O Lord: I said, Thou art my refuge and my portion in the land of the living." Millions of people exist in this world whom nobody loves and for whom nobody cares. They know there is no one who cares whether they live or die. It is today's great tragedy. David penned Psalm 142 during a period in his life when there was no one who would acknowledge knowing him. In his great depression he cried out, "There was no one that would know me . . . no man cared for my soul." So what did he do? Did he sit and brood about his unhappy plight? No; when all men rejected him, he turned to the one who would listen. He turned to God. He knew God was his refuge and friend.

When this unhappy chapter in his life ended and he was restored to more pleasant days, David unashamedly acknowledged his total dependence on God. This acknowledgment is a rare occurrence in our world. I have known people who went through the deep waters of rejection and fear and who cried out to God in helpless abandon. And when God delivered them, they were ashamed to acknowledge publicly the heartache and tears from which God had delivered them in answer to their desperate prayers during this time. God is glorified, and our hearts are glad when we testify to his deliverance in answer to our helpless cries.

Jeremiah proclaimed the gracious mercy of God, even to a people who had forsaken and forgotten God, and on whom God had pronounced judgment. Israel had been carried off into captivity; yet God looked down upon the misery of his sinful and rebellious people and made one of the most beautiful promises found in the Bible. It is filled with grace and compassion:

> For thus saith the Lord, That after seventy years
> be accomplished at Babylon I will visit you, and
> perform my good work toward you, in causing
> you to return to this place. For I know the
> thoughts that I think toward you, saith the Lord,
> Thoughts of peace, and not of evil, to give you
> an expected end. Then shall ye call upon me, and
> ye shall go and pray unto me, and I will hearken
> unto you. And ye shall seek me, and find me,
> when ye shall search for me with all your heart.
> (Jeremiah 29:10–13)

These are strange words. God had been spurned
and ridiculed by Israel; but instead of continuing
judgment, he planned peace and deliverance for his
rebellious people. Their deliverance, however, re-
quired wholehearted prayer. Persevering prayer is
the key to restoration.

The New Testament abounds with this same
idea. Paul spoke to the Romans about "continuing
instant in prayer" (Romans 12:12). To the Ephesians it was *"praying always* with all prayer and
supplication in the Spirit, and watching thereunto
with all perseverance and supplication for all
saints" (Ephesians 6:18). He urged the Colossians
to *"continue* in prayer." To help them understand
his teaching, he cited a young man as an example:
"Epaphras, who is one of you, a servant of Christ,
saluteth you, *always* labouring fervently for you *in*

prayers, that ye may stand perfect and complete in all the will of God" (Colossians 4:12). Paul told the Thessalonians simply to "pray *without ceasing*" (1 Thessalonians 5:17).

There are two kinds of prayer that relate to perseverance. One is our daily, planned time alone with the Lord, a time set aside for communion and fellowship with him through morning prayer and Bible reading. We must take pains to guard this time as precious and vital. Without it, we become powerless in our daily walk and service for him.

But there is another aspect of prayer that must be cultivated if we are to pray without ceasing. This is spontaneous prayer that bursts from our heart at any time of the day or night. Spontaneous prayer can be triggered by an unexpected joyful occurrence that causes praise to the Lord to well up in our soul. Or it can be an unexpected problem that causes us automatically to turn to him in prayer. We should come to the place in our growth in prayer where we spontaneously pray about everything. This prayer is unpremeditated, *impromptu*, spur-of-the-moment—almost a reflex action.

To persevere in prayer demands that we not give up. We should always pray and not faint (Luke 18:1). Jonah, for example, was about to be thrown overboard because the ship's crew had determined that he was the source of their trouble.

When he was at the end of his rope, he kept from completely losing heart by remembering the past goodness of God: "When my life was ebbing away, I remembered you, Lord, and my prayer rose to you, to your holy temple" (Jonah 2:7, NIV). Reflecting on God was good medicine for his flagging spirit. He thought of what God had done for him in the past and took courage. Our troubles should cause us to think about God and prompt us to call upon him.

David says the alternative to believing prayer is fainting. "I had fainted, unless I had believed to see the goodness of the Lord in the land of the living" (Psalm 27:13). You don't expect that sort of admission from the man who boldly slew Goliath; however, David's cry reveals that even strong men, valiant in battle, have their fainting spells. In David's depression his faith in God revived his fainting soul.

Paul adds his word of encouragement for the weary to persevere: "And let us not be weary in well doing: for in due season we shall reap, if we faint not" (Galatians 6:9). Jonah needed a backward glance to remember the past goodness of God. David believed in God's goodness here and now. Paul says we must wait on God, because some requests are not answered immediately but will be answered in the future.

The farmer doesn't expect to plant one day

and reap the next. Growing things take time to mature. Prayer is like that. Some prayers are answered immediately; some are not. Prayer is not like punching a button on a computer and getting an immediate electronic answer. Answers to prayer are never automatic; they often involve changes in ourselves or others which take time. You and I must acknowledge the wisdom of God in his timing. Let us determine to learn to pray fervently and persistently and not to give up.

11
Not Just Prayer, But Prayer *Plus*

BUT WE PRAYED TO OUR GOD
AND POSTED A GUARD
DAY AND NIGHT TO MEET THIS THREAT.

Nehemiah 4:9, NIV

SOME MONTHS AGO I was in a prayer meeting with a roomful of mission executives. We had spent the early hours of the morning in prayer for the various fields of the world and the needs of the missionaries in those areas. We had prayed for the unhindered sowing of the gospel seed, the receptivity of the hearers, and grace and strength for the sowers. It had been a good morning.

When it was about time to break for mid-

morning coffee, the leader suggested we spend a
few more minutes in prayer for each other. He
asked each person to share one personal prayer request with the person next to him; thus we would
finish our prayer time bearing up each other in
prayer. The man next to me asked me to pray that
he would lose weight. I was only too happy to do so
because I had recently had a struggle with this
problem myself. When we went to prayer again, I
asked the Lord to help him in this regard.

When we finished our prayer time, we went to
the table for coffee, tea, punch, and a few items to
nibble on. Then something happened that really
shocked me. I couldn't believe my eyes. The man
who had the weight problem made a bee-line for
the table. He scooped up a handful of peanuts and
in the other hand took a doughnut. He wolfed them
down in minutes, returned to the table and took
another handful of nuts and another doughnut,
covered with chocolate this time, and devoured
them with the same enthusiasm. It became plain to
me that my prayers for him were not going to be
answered.

Looking back on that event, I recall the words
of Jesus: "Watch and pray so that you will not fall
into temptation. The spirit is willing, but the body
is weak (Matthew 26:41, NIV). Jesus had found the
disciples sleeping, drained emotionally and worn
out physically. He spoke particularly to Peter,

warning him to be on the alert so that the forthcoming events should not take him by surprise and cause him to buckle under pressure and yield to temptation. Jesus knew the nature of Peter and the other disciples, and he knew the trials that were coming. Furthermore, Jesus knew the power of prayer. But his word to Peter was not only to pray, but also to be watchful and alert—on his guard. There is a time to pray and a time to watch. Both are necessary.

Recently I was talking to a man who had planned and directed a one-day conference. He was disappointed with the attendance. About half the number of people he'd expected had come. I asked him what he had *done* to make his hope for a larger crowd a reality. He said he had prayed and recruited prayer from others on behalf of the conference. I told him I was convinced that prayer was all-important. Then I asked what *else* he had done. He had, in fact, done very little else. Had he called the pastors of the city and asked them to announce the conference to their congregation? No. Had he asked if he could leave brochures describing the conference in the foyers of the churches? No. Had he made use of the Christian radio station in any way? No. Had he alerted the directors of various Christian organizations and encouraged them to come and bring their people? No. There were many other things he could have and should have done to follow up his prayer—like my friend with the weight problem. We should pray, then take the next step—avoid the doughnut table, call the pastors, or advertise in the newspapers. Jesus wanted Peter both *to watch* and *to pray*.

Recently I was asked to speak at the national convention of a Christian organization. My wife and I both went, and we had a marvelous week. It was held in a large, beautiful hotel that had almost everything. It had tennis courts, a golf course, swimming pools, exercise room, good food and a pleasant atmosphere. The one thing it did not have was soundproof rooms. The walls between the rooms were so thin that I could almost hear the guy's watch tick in the room next door. My wife and I usually retire early, because we like to get up early, but our neighbors next door were night people. Every night around midnight they came bouncing into their room laughing and joking. They would flip on the television and watch reruns of "Starsky and Hutch" or "Barretta" into the wee hours of morning. Each morning, however, at the early morning prayer meetings, they were always missing. They were also missing at the fellowship meeting around the breakfast table. They were missing at the praise and worship service after breakfast. About the time the mid-morning speaker was to begin, they would stumble into the auditorium, bleary and puffy-eyed, the pillow marks still on their faces. Possibly they had prayed on their way to the convention that they would get all God had for them during that week. Did they get it? Probably not. Was it God's fault? No. What was the problem? God was willing to answer their prayers. *They* were the problem. They should have taken steps to insure their attendance at the prayer meeting, the fellowship at the breakfast table, and the worship and praise. Their prayers should have been accompanied by common sense and discipline. God desires to bless us, but we must do what we can to be in his path of blessing. God wants our fellowship. Jesus died to make it possible for us to commune with God personally. We must do what we can to make that time of fellowship with him profitable.

I am the sort of person who most enjoys prayer time in the early morning in a quiet place where there are no distractions. One day, however, the neighborhood paperboy offered to deliver the morning paper free for six weeks. No obligation to buy; it was a circulation promotion scheme. I finally agreed. The next morning I was having my time of morning prayer and Bible reading when I heard an unfamiliar *kerthump* at the front door. The morning paper had arrived. Immediately my mind began to wander; "I wonder what's going on in the world this morning." I tried to continue my time with the Lord, but it was no use. My curiosity got the better of me. So I closed my Bible, went downstairs, got the paper and found out what was going on in the world. The following day I was enjoying my morning fellowship with God when *kerthump*—the morning paper arrived. Again my curiosity took over. So once again I closed the Bible, got the paper, and caught up on the morning news.

I saw what was happening, and I didn't like it. The next morning I cancelled the free delivery. I can hear some of you saying, "You should have been able to resist the temptation to read the paper. You should have been stronger in your resolve to maintain your quiet time." Of course I should have been, but that is the point—I wasn't. The simple solution was to eliminate the distraction. Asking God to give me an unhindered, unhurried, undistracted time of prayer while at the same time inviting the distraction to enter my mind would have been hypocrisy. It was my responsibility to take action, and I did.

Nehemiah was a man of prayer. His goal was to rebuild the wall around Jerusalem. When he heard of the sad state of his countrymen in Jerusalem, his first act was to pray:

The words of Nehemiah son of Hacaliah: In the month of Kislev in the twentieth year, while I was in the citadel of Susa, Hanai, one of my

brothers, came from Judah with some other
men, and I questioned them about the Jewish
remnant that survived the exile, and also about
Jerusalem.

They said to me, "Those who survived the exile and are back in the province are in great
trouble and disgrace. The wall of Jerusalem is
broken down, and its gates have been burned
with fire."

When I heard these things, I sat down and
wept. For some days I *mourned* and *fasted* and
prayed before the God of heaven. (Nehemiah
1:1–4, NIV)

Then Nehemiah had a chance to speak to the king,
and in his next step toward his goal, he did more
than pray.

In the month of Nisan in the twentieth year of
King Artaxerxes, when wine was brought for
him, I took the wine and gave it to the king. I
had not been sad in his presence before; so the
king asked me, "Why does your face look so sad
when you are not ill? This can be nothing but
sadness of heart."

I was very much afraid, but I said to the king,
"May the king live forever! Why should my face
not look sad when the city where my fathers are
buried lies in ruins, and its gates have been
destroyed by fire?"

The king said to me, "What is it you want?"

Then I prayed to the God of heaven, *and I answered the king*, "If it pleases the king and if your servant has found favor in his sight, let him send me to the city in Judah where my fathers are buried so that I can rebuild it." (Nehemiah 2:1-5, NIV)

Nehemiah was a man of prayer, but he also boldly told the king about his needs when God gave him the opportunity.

When Nehemiah was attacked in the midst of the wall-building program, he proved once again that he was a man of action as well as prayer.

But when Sanballat, Tobiah, the Arabs, the Ammonites and the men of Ashdod heard that the repairs to Jerusalem's walls had gone ahead and that the gaps were being closed, they were very angry. They all plotted together to come and fight against Jerusalem and stir up trouble against it. But we prayed to our God *and posted a guard day and night* to meet this threat. (Nehemiah 4:7-9, NIV)

They prayed *and posted a guard*.

Prayer could injure our personal growth if it were to take the place of all human action. The development of Christian character is enhanced by human struggle. If all our needs were supplied through prayer with no effort of our own, we would become weak and soft. Imagine someone praying, "God, mow the lawn." "God, clean my room." "God, teach me the book of Romans." God is not our slave. Prayer is no excuse for sloth.

Had Nehemiah set a watch without praying, he would have offended God. He would have asserted his independence from God and confidence in his own ability to handle the matter. He would have been in trouble, because "God opposes the proud" (1 Peter 5:5, NIV). Nehemiah knew he had to pray *and* work. Had he prayed without setting a watch, however, he would have demonstrated the folly of idleness.

One of the clearest examples of this truth is found in the book of Acts. On his way to Rome, the apostle Paul was in a great storm at sea. Luke tells us Paul had a direct promise from God that not one life aboard the ship would be lost:

> When neither sun nor stars appeared for many days and the storm continued raging, we finally gave up all hope of being saved.
>
> After the men had gone a long time without food, Paul stood up before them and said: "Men, you should have taken my advice not to sail from Crete; then you would have spared yourselves this damage and loss. But now I urge you to keep up your courage, because not one of you

will be lost; only the ship will be destroyed. Last
night an angel of the God whose I am and whom
I serve stood beside me and said, 'Do not be
afraid, Paul. You must stand trial before Caesar;
and God has graciously given you the lives of all
who sail with you.' So keep up your courage,
men, for I have faith in God that it will happen
just as he told me." (Acts 27:20–25, NIV)

The clear promise from God was, "There shall be
no loss of any man's life." Paul believed that promise and claimed it for himself and the rest of his
companions. But did Paul chide the men for using
their common sense in taking appropriate means to
help ensure their safety? When he saw them testing
the depth of the water, did he berate them for not
believing him? Or did he tell them to stop casting
out the anchors, throwing the grain overboard,
loosening the rudder bands, or raising the foresail
to the wind? No, of course not. These were common practices for a ship in danger. Paul was an experienced man in these matters, having been "in
journeyings often, in perils of waters" (2 Corinthians 11:26). He had been in three shipwrecks and
had spent a night and a day in the ocean (2 Corinthians 11:25). Rather than complain to the men
regarding their lack of faith, Paul probably ap-
plauded their efforts. We must not tempt God and
presume on his goodness through our laziness or

lack of common sense. I'm sure Paul would have commended Nehemiah, who, after praying, "posted a guard against them day and night."

One of the classic statements of this principle in the New Testament is in Paul's letter to the Philippians:

> Therefore, my dear friends, as you have always obeyed—not only in my presence, but now much more in my absence—continue to work out your salvation with fear and trembling, for it is God who works in you to will and to act according to his good purpose. (Philippians 2:12-13, NIV)

Paul exhorts the Philippian Christians to exercise diligence in their Christian life because God is at work in them. He tells them to work because God is at work.

God stands ready to bless our diligence if we exercise it in total dependence on him. Prayer declares our total dependence. On our knees, we demonstrate that our confidence is in God. Paul testifies of this dependence: "I can do everything *through him who gives me strength*" (Philippians 4:13, NIV). His confidence was in God, but this confidence led him to work harder: "But by the grace of God I am what I am, and his grace to me was not without effect. No, *I worked harder than all of them*—yet not I, but the grace of God that was with me" (1 Corinthians 15:10, NIV). Prayer and human effort found a beautiful balance in Paul's life.

There are a number of places in the New Testament where Jesus alerts us to our duty to watch and pray. In Mark 13:33–36 he says that sloth brings spiritual blindness to the signs of his second coming, and that watchfulness in prayer is the antidote to this blindness. In Luke 21:34–36, Jesus warns of this same blindness and says that gluttony, drunkenness, and worldliness hinder watchfulness. He teaches that victory over these enemies comes through watching and praying.

The apostle Peter was a man of prayer; he understood its power. He said on one occasion that he would give himself "continually to prayer" (Acts 6:4). He exhorted husbands and wives to live together in love and harmony, "that your prayer be not hindered" (1 Peter 3:7).

But Peter does not neglect human effort. When he speaks of the things that lead to fruitful lives and a true knowledge of our Lord Jesus Christ, he says,

> For this very reason, make every effort to add to your faith goodness; and to goodness, knowledge; and to knowledge, self-control; and to self-control, perseverance; and to perseverance, godliness; and to godliness, brotherly kindness; and to brotherly kindness, love. For if you

possess these qualities in increasing measure,
they will keep you from being ineffective and
unproductive in your knowledge of our Lord
Jesus Christ. (2 Peter 1:5–8, NIV)

Peter gives us a list of Christian virtues that will
help us overcome the things Jesus warned
against— blindness, sloth, gluttony, drunkenness,
and worldliness.

These passages, as well as many others, teach
that prayer, to be effective, must be accompanied
by our diligence, watchfulness, and God-directed
effort.

12
Epilogue

ONE DAY JESUS WAS PRAYING
IN A CERTAIN PLACE. WHEN HE FINISHED,
ONE OF HIS DISCIPLES SAID TO HIM,
"LORD, TEACH US TO PRAY,
JUST AS JOHN TAUGHT HIS DISCIPLES."

Luke 11:1, NIV

JESUS' DISCIPLES HAD a request. They had seen the master praying, and their hearts were touched; they wanted to learn to pray, too. So one of them asked Jesus to teach them to pray, not realizing that in making the request they were, in fact, partially answering it.

Jesus responded by giving them a model prayer which contained spiritual principles that would lead them into a rich prayer life. But their simple request, "Lord, teach us to pray," was the beginning —the initiative—that started the whole process.

We, too, must start here in the life of prayer— where we are. We can waste a lot of time getting prepared to pray, or waiting on the right mood to strike us, or learning how to pray by reading books and listening to sermons on prayer, but sooner or later we must *pray*— and that beginning prayer may be as simple as, "Lord, help me." What matters most is that we cry out to the Lord, and that we cry from our hearts.

That humble cry for help opens the gate to the garden of prayer. The path we enter after the gate has been opened may be narrow at first, but as we follow it we find that it widens out into a beautiful garden graced with shade trees and flowers; their names are confession, praise, thanksgiving, intercession, and petition. The whole garden is watered with the dew of humility.

We will eventually find ourselves coming to this garden more frequently and staying longer. As we explore its delights, we discover new expanses and surprises unfolding before us. There are comfortable benches where we can sit down and talk to our heavenly Father in ever-increasing intimacy. He tells us how to cultivate the garden so that its trees and lawns and shrubs will grow luxuriantly, and we learn that the care of the garden is a joint responsibility which we share with him. We find refuge in its shady glens from the burning heat of the day, and our souls which were dry and parched are restored and refreshed.

A sense of awe and wonder, such as we used to have in childhood, begins to reassert itself as we sense the majesty of the Master himself. His presence creates the beauty we feel. We find that we are changed and humbled, and that we see reality more clearly than before coming here.

Though we may enter this garden with heavy and burdened hearts, we soon feel strong arms lift the burdens and apply the balm of Gilead to our bruised and torn backs.

Dwelling in the garden of prayer has a transforming effect on our spirits. First we realize our shabbiness and our stained appearance. When we tell the Master about this ugliness, he takes it away, cleanses us, and clothes us with new apparel.

We emerge from the garden with its fragrance still upon us. Our spirits have absorbed the harmony of this precious place, and as a result we find we can live harmoniously with others. We are stronger, wiser, and gentler than we were before we began to frequent the garden of prayer. We are strong to do the work at hand—the planting of other gardens in lives that are dry and withered.

It all starts with the first step—the cry, "Lord, teach me. . . ."